THE SECRET OF THE SEVEN PILLARS

*Building Your Life on God's Wisdom
from the Book of Proverbs*

Dedication

To my wife, Jennifer, who equally invested in this work. To Makaela, Alyssa, Matthew and Amanda and to your children and your children's children for a hundred generations—this book is for all of you. I am abundantly grateful to my friends who shared the refinement of this work: Leigh Bashor, Michael Callen, Phil Sommerville, and my beloved mother and father.

This is the Lord's doing; it is marvelous in our eyes.
—Psalm 118:23

D.A.B.
2007

Contents

Preface

The book of Proverbs contains *real treasure* — not the kind that disappears after we die or gives us false assurance of self-worth while we're alive — but the type of treasure that provides rich fulfillment and purpose while we're alive, as well as rewards after we pass on.

This book is designed to pour these treasures into your life by connecting the biblical truths about wisdom from both the Old and New Testament. James, the disciple and half-brother of Christ, defines the *framework* of godly wisdom as having a *foundation* of purity and *seven key attributes*: "the wisdom that comes from heaven is first of all pure; then peace-loving, considerate, submissive, full of mercy and good fruit, impartial and sincere" (James 3:17). When writing Proverbs nearly a thousand years earlier, King Solomon described wisdom as having seven pillars: "Wisdom has built her house; she has hewn out its *seven pillars*" (Proverbs 9:1). This book delivers unique wisdom principles for living a godly life in the twenty-first century by using James's unique list of seven key wisdom attributes to organize many of the key verses in Proverbs.

By taking one week to focus on each of the seven pillars of wisdom, this book will help establish the solid framework of godly wisdom in your life, career and family. Five devotions are provided for every week that explore facets of each of the seven pillars using the rich and challenging proverbs relevant to each pillar.

It is my hope that you are challenged and encouraged as you discover how the timeless truths of wisdom can change your life.

Introduction

One early Saturday morning Mike and I set out with plans to build a bridge across a creek that runs through our property. Mike, my brother-in-law, had a background in pool construction, and I had some carpentry experience, so we thought we could put together a halfway decent plan for building the bridge. We started with a pre-built redwood bridge that was about 12 feet long and 4 feet wide and planned to secure it to tree roots on each side of the creek using large lag bolts. Neither of us was a construction expert, but we had at least some faith in our ability and believed we could make a bridge that would stay in place—at least for a few years. We had ninety percent ambition mixed with ten percent skill and thought this would be enough for our weekend project. After all, we weren't building a bridge for cars, but just for kids and pets!

About an hour into the process my neighbor Ray wandered over to watch the fun. Ray had over forty years' experience in residential construction and was nicknamed "the best carpenter in town." He stood there watching for a few minutes—patiently observing as the steam of his morning coffee rolled up his face. Then, after minutes of silence, he humbly offered these words:

> You know, if I were building this bridge, I would buy a couple of 20-foot long, 6-inch by 8-inch beams of treated lumber, a thousand pounds of concrete, concrete post tubes for forming piers and anchoring hardware for securing everything together. I would set these 250-pound concrete piers on each side of the creek, with each about five feet apart, set above the high-water line where the creek water rises each winter. Next, I'd secure the two 20-foot beams like railroad tracks spanning the creek with the ends mounted into each concrete pier using sturdy hardware. Then I'd put your pre-made bridge on top of the two beams and secure it using 8-inch lag bolts. This way you'll never need to rebuild the bridge, and it will be strong enough to withstand the floods that come about every three years.

Although we were pridefully reluctant at first, we followed his advice, and the bridge still stands today. It has survived years of use, intense rains and floods (including being submerged a few times) and even withstood a tree that crashed on top of it during a storm. This would not have been the case had we built the bridge the way we had originally planned.

In many ways this story relates to our lives. Think of it—as mere humans are we really suited for making our own choices about matters of morality, values and integrity? So many people believe they can *build* their own lives by relying on their own moral compass rather than God's. They often depend on relativistic "what works for you must be okay" types of values and make choices that will inevitably result in negative consequences. But God and His Word stand by humbly, waiting patiently, desiring to coach us as we build our lives by making choices every day. Some of us listen; even fewer listen and obey. But those of us who *act upon God's Word* will end up with a life that will not be shaken—even by the worst of storms—just as Christ explained in the parable of the wise and foolish builders:

> Therefore everyone who hears these words of mine and puts them into practice is like a wise man who built his house on the rock. The rain came down, the streams rose, and the winds blew and beat against that house; yet it did not fall, because it had its foundation on the rock. But everyone who hears these words of mine and does not put them into practice is like a foolish man who built his house on sand. The rain came down, the streams rose, and the winds blew and beat against that house, and it fell with a great crash. When Jesus had finished saying these things, the crowds were amazed at his teaching, because he taught as one who had authority, and not as their teachers of the law (Matthew 7:24-29).

An interesting parallel is found in Proverbs 1:20-33:

> Wisdom calls aloud in the street, she raises her voice in the public squares; at the head of the noisy streets she cries out, in the gateways of the city she makes her speech: "How long will you simple ones love your simple ways? How long will mockers delight in mockery and fools hate knowledge? If you had responded to my rebuke, I would have poured out my heart to you and made my thoughts known to you. But since you rejected me when I called and no one gave heed when I stretched out my hand, since you ignored all my advice and would not accept my rebuke, I in turn will laugh at your disaster; I will mock when calamity overtakes you—when calamity overtakes you like a storm, when disaster sweeps over you like a whirlwind, when distress and trouble over-whelm you. Then they will call to me but I will not answer; they will look for me but will not find me. Since they hated knowledge and did not choose to fear the Lord, since they would not accept my advice and spurned my rebuke, they will eat the fruit of their ways and be filled with the fruit

of their schemes. For the waywardness of the simple will kill them, and the complacency of fools will destroy them; but whoever listens to me will live in safety and be at ease, without fear of harm."

Do we really *know* what's best for our lives? Can we effectively make decisions about matters of morality and values? Or should we rely on the Master Builder who has given us *His plans*? Those plans are found in the Bible, which promises that we will have a *blessed* life if we choose to apply it in our lives.

Following the wisdom principles laid out in Proverbs will ensure that we build a solid foundation for virtually every significant part of our lives. All of us are building our lives *one building block at a time*, and each building block can be set upon a solid, lasting foundation or on a shifting, sinking one.

What advice would King Solomon, author of most of Proverbs and the wisest man who ever lived (after Jesus), offer if you asked him how to build the foundation of your family, business or ministry? What would be the very first things he would recommend for your "Mission, Vision and Values" statement? Fortunately these precepts have already been set out for us in the timeless wisdom the Lord gave to us in the book of Proverbs:

- "Kings detest wrongdoing, for a throne is established through righteousness" (16:12).
- "Remove the dross from the silver, and out comes material for the silversmith; remove the wicked from the king's presence, and his throne will be established through righteousness" (25:4-5).
- "By justice a king gives a country stability, but one who is greedy for bribes tears it down" (29:4).
- "If a ruler listens to lies, all his officials become wicked" (29:12).
- "If a king judges the poor with fairness, his throne will always be secure" (29:14).

Here are some examples of how we can directly apply these principles in our home, ministry or workplace:

- Base your very foundation upon righteousness. This should be your overriding principle for all that you do.
- Be sure your close advisors and friends are persons of integrity, and your home, business and ministry will have a solid foundation.
- Do not be led astray by lies or take bribes because these destructive forces will tear down your home, business or ministry and corrupt your closest followers.
- Love the poor and judge them with fairness, which will result in your family, business and ministry having a stable and lasting impact.

The Seven Pillars of Wisdom

Godly wisdom has a foundation of purity and seven pillars that support its structure: "Wisdom has built her house; she has hewn out its *seven pillars*" (Proverbs 9:1). Purity is regarded as the very foundation of wisdom's house and the most essential part, because James lists purity as "first of all" in the list of seven wisdom traits that follow. In his commentary on James, Barton (1992, p. 87) remarks that the term "first" in this passage indicates that "this (purity) is the main characteristic and a *key to the others*, not just number one." For this reason purity is covered in its own section in this book.

What about the seven pillars of wisdom that are built on the foundation of purity? King Solomon, who authored most of Proverbs, does not explain what they are. While many explanations have been sought, James the disciple defined godly wisdom a thousand years after King Solomon penned this proverb. Surprisingly, his definition included *seven key characteristics*:

Pillar 1: Peace-loving
Pillar 2: Considerate
Pillar 3: Submissive
Pillar 4: Merciful

Pillar 5: Fruitful
Pillar 6: Impartial
Pillar 7: Sincere

Looking at these seven pillars in context, James writes:

> Who is wise and understanding among you? Let him show it by his good life, by deeds done in the humility that comes from wisdom. But if you harbor bitter envy and selfish ambition in your hearts, do not boast about it or deny the truth. Such "wisdom" does not come down from heaven but is earthly, unspiritual, of the devil. For where you have envy and selfish ambition, there you find disorder and every evil practice. ***But the wisdom that comes from heaven is first of all pure; then peace-loving, considerate, submissive, full of mercy and good fruit, impartial and sincere.*** Peacemakers who sow in peace raise a harvest of righteousness (James 3:13-18).

Proverbs establishes that there are seven pillars of wisdom; James defines what they are a thousand years later! (For those readers interested in a more detailed explanation of these seven pillars, please see the appendix.) Proverbs includes thirty-one chapters and 915 verses that span a wide assortment of topics. Remarkably, however, when James's seven pillars are used to organize the 915 verses, over half fall nicely into one or more pillars (see the appendix for a listing of proverbs that have been categorized into the seven pillars).

Over the next thirty-five days we will explore these seven pillars of wisdom gleaned from the book of Proverbs. Consider this a book of construction plans for your life from our Master Builder. If we follow these plans, these seven pillars of wisdom will give our lives an unshakable foundation and allow us to experience God's best for our lives. As you spend five days exploring and applying each of these themes, it is my prayer that they will become the pillars of your life that lead to godly character and the realization of God's best plans for all He has in store for you.

Wisdom and the Book of Proverbs

James defines godly wisdom as having a foundation of purity and seven key traits of wisdom—but how does this tie into the book of Proverbs, which was written at least a thousand years earlier? The book of Proverbs is a mysterious book. In fact, some view it as a somewhat scattered collection of "truth snippets" that apply to a wide variety of topics. While the book is somewhat wide and varying in what it covers and how, it is nonetheless *complete*. The 915 verses are nicely divided into thirty-one chapters which some find convenient for dividing into daily readings for every month. It's also a tremendously broad book—covering virtually every topic dealing with morality, ethics and integrity.

The book of Proverbs is also *alive*. As part of the works of Scripture, Proverbs has the endorsement of Hebrews 4:12-13:

> For the word of God is living and active. Sharper than any double-edged sword, it penetrates even to dividing soul and spirit, joints and marrow; it judges the thoughts and attitudes of the heart. Nothing in all creation is hidden from God's sight. Everything is uncovered and laid bare before the eyes of him to whom we must give account.

Some proverbs make obvious sense; others are more obscure and need to be unraveled through careful study. Yet others are hidden as riddles. No matter the form, they all share the infinite power of God's Word.

Most of the book of Proverbs was written by King Solomon, David's son. Solomon was the wisest man (excluding Christ, of course) ever to walk the face of this planet. Solomon was endowed with the *gift* of wisdom because he asked for it and God honored his request; it's really that simple. He wasn't born with a giant brain or some uniquely gifted way of viewing the world. Rather, Solomon was granted the gift of wisdom by God *because he made a choice to pursue this gift over the "other options."*

Early in King Solomon's reign, God appeared to Solomon and said: "Ask for whatever you want me to give you" (2 Chronicles

1:7). That's quite an invitation—the God of the universe offering Solomon *anything* he wanted! Solomon chose wisely and asked God for wisdom above all else:

> Solomon answered God, "You have shown great kindness to David my father and have made me king in his place. Now, Lord God, let your promise to my father David be confirmed, for you have made me king over a people who are as numerous as the dust of the earth. Give me wisdom and knowledge, that I may lead this people, for who is able to govern this great people of yours?" God said to Solomon, "Since this is your heart's desire and you have not asked for wealth, riches or honor, nor for the death of your enemies, and since you have not asked for a long life but for wisdom and knowledge to govern my people over whom I have made you king, therefore wisdom and knowledge will be given you. And I will also give you wealth, riches and honor, such as no king who was before you ever had and none after you will have (2 Chronicles 1:8-12).

This single choice made by one man over three thousand years ago changed the course of world history. Solomon's answer ultimately resulted in his writing the book of Proverbs which captures much of the boundless wisdom bestowed upon him by God.

This "transaction" that occurred between God and Solomon was not a one-time opportunity issued to a single person. In fact, we are all offered similar opportunities in our lives today: "If any of you lacks wisdom, he should ask God, who gives generously to all without finding fault, and it will be given to him. But when he asks, he must believe and not doubt, because he who doubts is like a wave of the sea, blown and tossed by the wind" (James 1:5-7). God offers us His wisdom for leading our daily lives, but it's our job to ask for it *and* receive it. We do this by prayer and consulting His Word.

As a result of Solomon's choice to select wisdom, a process was put into place that ultimately gave us the book of Proverbs. When Proverbs was compiled, it was designed as a training guide for Israel's leaders (Hubbard, 1989, p. 12, 26). It included 915 sayings marked by shortness, sensibility and "salt" so as to have a certain "bite" when read. The opening of the book (in Proverbs 1:1-7) lays out the main ingredients that define and differentiate wisdom:

> The proverbs of Solomon son of David, king of Israel: for attaining wisdom and discipline; for understanding words of insight; for acquiring a disciplined and prudent life, doing what is right and just and fair; for giving prudence to the simple, knowledge and discretion to the young—let the wise listen and add to their learning, and let the discerning get guidance—for understanding proverbs and parables, the sayings and riddles of the wise. The fear of the Lord is the beginning of knowledge, but fools despise wisdom and discipline.

Consider now the key elements in the opening passage of Proverbs. Not only does this passage share what the book is about, it shares how it can transform the lives of those who adopt its truths:

- attaining wisdom and discipline
- understanding words of insight
- acquiring a disciplined and prudent life
- doing what is right and just and fair
- giving prudence to the simple
- giving knowledge and discretion to the young

Have you ever seen a more powerful promise offered by *any other book ever written*? One that promises wisdom, discipline, understanding, the tools for living a prudent life, learning how to be right and fair, gaining prudence and knowledge?

The Differences Between Worldly Wisdom and Godly Wisdom

There are many smart, knowledgeable and wise people on this earth. But can someone really have *true wisdom* without God—the very one who breathed life into mankind? The shocking answer is no. The Bible says we *cannot even start* to gain true wisdom without first acknowledging God. This is because the gap between worldly human wisdom, understanding and knowledge compared to true godly wisdom and understanding is immeasurable: "For my thoughts are not your thoughts, neither are your ways my ways," declares the Lord. "As the heavens are higher than the earth, so are my ways higher than your ways and my thoughts than your thoughts" (Isaiah 55:8-9).

For people to claim true wisdom and understanding without God is like my five-year-old son claiming to know how to build the space shuttle. Let's remember that God is the maker of humankind and not the other way around: "Shall what is formed say to him who formed it, 'He did not make me?' Can the pot say of the potter, 'He knows nothing?'" (Isaiah 29:16).

While people can aspire to learn and grow in all types of wisdom, knowledge and understanding, growing in true wisdom requires starting with God. The Bible says we cannot *even begin* to have true wisdom or understanding unless we connect directly with the wisdom's source:

- "Do not deceive yourselves. If any one of you thinks he is wise by the standards of this age, he should become a 'fool' so that he may become wise. For the wisdom of this world is foolishness in God's sight. As it is written: 'He catches the wise in their craftiness'; and again, 'The Lord knows that the thoughts of the wise are futile'" (1 Corinthians 3:18-20).
- "The fear of the Lord is the beginning of knowledge, but fools despise wisdom and discipline" (Proverbs 1:7).
- "My son, if you accept my words and store up my commands within you, turning your ear to wisdom and applying your heart to understanding, and if you call out for insight and cry aloud for understanding, and if you look for it as for silver and search for it as for hidden treasure, then you will understand the fear of the Lord and find the knowledge of God. *For the Lord gives wisdom, and from his mouth come knowledge and understanding*" (Proverbs 2:1-6).

So many people overlook this principle—that true wisdom can only be attained from God. And sadly many reach the end of their lives having "done it their way," only to realize they've been playing checkers on a chess board. True wisdom, values and success are attained by pursuing and knowing God, His will and His purpose for our lives—and it's never too late to do this. Biblical examples of late bloomers abound!

So—what's the big difference between worldly wisdom and godly wisdom? It's all about perspective: worldly wisdom understands and depends on the *now*; godly wisdom has an *eternal* perspective. Worldly wisdom can show you how to attain wealth; godly wisdom cautions us that wealth is only temporary and should be used as a resource rather than security or spent predominantly on our own lavish enjoyment. Worldly wisdom will teach you how to find and enjoy pleasures; godly wisdom will teach you how to find true, lasting joy and peace and will even send treasures ahead for our future life in eternity.

Purity:
The Foundation of Wisdom

Because you're reading this book and this book is about God's Word, you are privy to some of God's *secrets*—some you already know; some you may discover for the very first time; and some secrets you think you already understand will be unveiled to you in a totally new way. One of the interesting things about godly wisdom is that most of it is really quite basic. Much of God's wisdom has already been laid out in His Word. It is not hidden in lofty riddles, tucked away in secret codes or whispered among a select few in elitist groups (for example, see 1 Corinthians 1:13– 2:16). The shame is that many people choose to walk their own way, rather than following God's, and end up with half-fulfilled, half-utilized lives as a result.

One of the "major secrets" I mentioned above is contained in this section on purity. Quite simply it's this: God has special servants— those who listen to His prompting and do His bidding. From Mother Teresa and Billy Graham to everyday believers, God has a *special relationship* with those who follow Him daily by locking onto the path of purity.

Living a Pure and Upright Life Can Put You on God's "Short List" of Preferred Servants

Proverbs 3:32 declares: "For the Lord detests a perverse man but *takes the upright into his confidence*." What an invitation! How would you like to gain the confidence and trust of the One who created the entire universe? The One who framed the first man and gave him His first breath? Does this sound like an honor? Perhaps honor is an understatement! Likewise, how can the God of the entire universe take a fallen, sinful person *into His confidence*?

Have no misunderstanding. Being an upright person does not mean being perfect—it means being upright. In fact, the original language for this term contains the idea of "being straight" and "not twisted or bent." When professional ice skaters perform, their goal is to *stay upright* until their performance ends. If they fall, they get right back up. Proverbs 24:16 declares the same goal for our lives: "*Though a righteous man falls seven times, he rises again*, but the wicked are brought down by calamity."

Biblical history gives us many real-life examples of not perfect, yet upright people. David was referred to as "a man after God's own heart" in 1 Samuel 13:14; yet David fell into an affair. But God still took David *into His confidence*. Jeremiah was depressed, Jonah ran away from God, Paul murdered, Martha worried too much, and Elijah burned out. All these people fell but came back upright until their performance, their lives, ended. God used them and brought them into His confidence.

Being upright before God requires both *position* and *lifestyle*. Faith in Christ changes our *position* before God (John 3:36). If we receive Christ, our position before God is changed from "condemned" to "child" (John 1:12, 3:16-19). This happens the moment we receive Christ into our hearts. Living an *upright lifestyle*, however, takes time. It also takes obedience, discipline and sometimes *pain and suffering*. As we grow deeper in our relationship with Christ, God slowly purges the sin from our lives and exchanges it with upright patterns of living, full of grace and peace.

Heartache and trials in life are sometimes God's tools to purify us so we can be used by Him on even greater levels (for example, James 1:2-5, Romans 5:3-5, Hebrews 12:5-13). When God stretches us during these times, it's important that we "suffer warmly," rather than growing cold toward Him. We need to soften our hearts and let God move within us—changing us from within as the pain paves the way. When we are going through difficult times and God is shaping and molding us, I believe He will actually shorten the painful experience if we submit our lives and hearts to the lessons He wants us to learn.

No matter what tools God uses to bring purity into our lives, they all have the same goal: to make us *more like Christ.* As we grow in Him and faithfully submit to each lesson He brings our way, God prepares us for even greater ministry and outreach opportunities. As we progress along this path, God takes *us*—the fallen people that we are—into His confidence to do His good works:

If a man cleanses himself from the latter [wickedness and godless living], he will be an instrument for noble purposes, made holy, useful to the Master and prepared to do any good work (2 Timothy 2:21).

The Lord confides in those who fear him; he makes his covenant known to them (Psalm 25:14).

I no longer call you servants, because a servant does not know his master's business. Instead, I have called you friends, for everything that I learned from my Father I have made known to you. You did not choose me, but I chose you and appointed you to go and bear fruit—fruit that will last. Then the Father will give you whatever you ask in my name. This is my command: Love each other (John 15:15-17).

Proverbs and the Path of Purity

There is a precious treasure in life that few people ever discover. It is to daily seek and follow divine direction for the right path to take in our lives. The impact of doing this will determine our direction in life over time and will ultimately lead us to our final destiny. Part of the divine direction we can receive from God is through prayer. Another part has already been delivered to us by God through His Word. And a lot of what can give us daily direction in His Word can be found in the book of Proverbs! Proverbs instructs us to find and follow God's *paths* and describes God's *way* for those who make a conscious daily choice to walk in God's path for their lives.

Because Proverbs is a divine and inspired book of the Bible, it is *timeless* and *alive* (Hebrews 4:12). Perhaps this is why I never fail to find new treasure each time I read it. It is full of complexities, challenges and even riddles. If I could summarize the entire book into a neat and tidy description, I would put it this way: All of Proverbs— its 915 verses and thirty-one chapters—is about *avoiding the evil path and actively pursuing the good path*. It is not about living a static or idle religious life. The book of Proverbs is designed to steer a *life in motion* toward doing the good that God put us here to do.

Throughout this life in motion we all take "paths" or "ways." These paths can be full of hills, potholes, slippery slopes, challenges, weather, darkness, bandits and blessings. To those who choose the way of righteousness, their paths will be marked by the same landscape as those who choose evil—the same hills, sunlight, gloomy days—but they are following very different paths. The path of the righteous includes special circumstances that are pre-arranged by God (Ephesians 2:8-10), timely blessings (Galatians 6:9), eternal rewards (Matthew 5-6) and the assurance that the challenges faced along the path occur for the good of those who love Him (Romans 8:28) and they will ultimately serve our own good if we are patient and endure (James 1:2-5 and 2 Corinthians 4:16-18).

Many have bought into the myth that God's laws, rules and precepts constrain us and keep us from enjoying the life we want to lead. The reality, however, is the opposite: these ways are in place to bless us. As stated in James, "But the man who looks intently into the perfect law that gives freedom, and continues to do this, not forgetting what he has heard, but doing it—he will be blessed in what he does" (James 1:25). Those who practice God's laws will enjoy blessed lives, not constrained, unfulfilled ones. Jesus has promised to be our *Good* Shepherd and to give us life *to the fullest* (John 10:10-11). The very Creator of life knows how to give us the best life possible, and much of this can only be accomplished by living our lives according to the standards He's already laid out clearly in His Word. Following these guideposts along our way in life keeps us on the righteous path He desires for our lives.

The book of Proverbs uses the term "way" or "path" forty-four times. This is more than any other book in the Bible, including the book of Psalms (a book roughly five times the length of Proverbs). Why is this so important? Because the way we choose to live is *all we have*—it is the sum of our entire life. Our way reflects our choices and their related consequences, our character, and ultimately it determines where we will end up in life. Quite simply our way is everything. Take in now what Proverbs says about our way:

Our Way Determines Our Safety and Protection

- "For the *waywardness* of the simple will kill them, and the complacency of fools will destroy them; but whoever listens to me will live in safety and be at ease, without fear of harm" (1:32-33).
- "He holds victory in store for the upright, he is a shield to those whose walk is blameless, for he guards the *course* of the just and protects the *way* of his faithful ones. Then you will understand what is right and just and fair—every *good path*. For wisdom will enter your heart, and knowledge will be pleasant to your soul. Discretion will protect you, and understanding will guard you. Wisdom will save you from the ways of wicked men, from men whose words are perverse, who leave the *straight paths* to walk in *dark ways*, who delight in doing wrong and rejoice in

the perverseness of evil, whose *paths* are crooked and who are devious in their *ways*" (2:7-15)

- "Then you will go on your *way* in safety, and your foot will not stumble" (3:23).
- "I guide you in the *way* of wisdom and lead you along *straight paths*. When you walk, your steps will not be hampered; when you run, you will not stumble" (4:11-12).
- "Let your eyes look straight ahead, fix your gaze directly before you. Make level *paths* for your feet and take only ways that are firm. Do not swerve to the right or the left; keep your foot from evil" (4:25-27).
- "The man of integrity walks securely, but he who takes *crooked paths* will be found out" (10:9).
- "The *way* of the Lord is a refuge for the righteous, but it is the ruin of those who do evil" (10:29).
- "There is a *way* that seems right to a man, but in the end it leads to death" (14:12).
- "A man who strays from the *path* of understanding comes to rest in the company of the dead" (21:16).
- "In the *paths* of the wicked lie thorns and snares, but he who guards his soul stays far from them" (22:5).
- "Do not make friends with a hot-tempered man, do not associate with one easily angered, or you may learn his *ways* and get yourself ensnared" (22:24-25).
- "He whose walk is blameless is kept safe, but he whose *ways* are perverse will suddenly fall" (28:18).

All of these proverbs speak to the importance of taking the *right path*. Proverbs 4:25-27 speaks the most directly on this topic. The Geneva Version translates this verse in a compelling way: "Let thine eyes behold the right, and let thine eyelids direct thy way before thee. Ponder the path of thy feet, and let all thy ways be ordered aright. Turn not to the right hand, nor to the left, but remove thy foot from evil."

In this verse the term "path" in the original language means a "rutted path," such as that which would be used for drawing a wagon or cart. A rutted path is one that has two tracks embedded in the surface that help "keep us in the tracks" or stay in the course that is best for our lives. For God's best to emerge in our lives, we need to stay focused by walking in the way He has called us. We need to actively find His way for our lives and order our steps daily after His way. Two of the best ways to do this (as suggested by this verse) are to *keep our eyes on Him* and *avoid getting sidetracked.*

Walking in the way of righteousness does not guarantee bad things will never happen. But living an upright life *does* mean you will spare yourself from the unnecessary dangers and pitfalls that *would have* occurred by living the *other way.* As we go about living our lives, circumstances become interconnected. One thing leads to another. It's a much better idea to stay on the safe track. When I find myself on the wrong road, I find it's easiest to "get back on track" by making a *resolution of will* to turn around and start heading the right way.

Our Way Determines Our Direction in Life—for Now and Eternity

- "In all your *ways* acknowledge him, and he will make your *paths straight*" (3:6).
- "The *path* of the righteous is like the first gleam of dawn, shining ever brighter till the full light of day. But the *way* of the wicked is like deep darkness; they do not know what makes them stumble" (4:18-19).
- "The righteousness of the blameless makes a *straight way* for them, but the wicked are brought down by their own wickedness" (11:5).
- "There is a *way* that seems right to a man, but in the end it leads to death" (14:12).
- "The *path* of life leads upward for the wise to keep him from going down to the grave" (15:24).
- "Train a child in the *way* he should go, and when he is old he will not turn from it" (22:6).
- "But since you rejected me when I called and no one gave heed when I stretched out my hand, since you ignored all my advice and would not accept my rebuke, I in turn will laugh at your disaster; I will mock when calamity overtakes

you—when calamity overtakes you like a storm, when disaster sweeps over you like a whirlwind, when distress and trouble overwhelm you. Then they will call to me but I will not answer; they will look for me but will not find me. Since they hated knowledge and did not choose to fear the Lord, since they would not accept my advice and spurned my rebuke, they will eat the fruit of their ways and be filled with the fruit of their schemes" (1:24-31).

How important is it that we stay in the way He has marked for our lives by walking in obedience to His Word? Consider some of King David's last words shared with his son, Solomon, when he was passing down his kingdom: "And you, my son Solomon, acknowledge the God of your father, and serve Him with wholehearted devotion and with a willing mind, for the Lord searches every heart and understands every motive behind the thoughts. If you seek him, he will be found by you; but if you forsake him, he will reject you forever" (1 Chronicles 28:9).

Our Way Determines Our Consequences (Negative or Positive)

Proverbs teaches that our way can determine much about our lives, including:

- The **difficulty** of our lives: "Good understanding wins favor, but the *way* of the unfaithful is hard" (13:15); "The Lord detests the *way* of the wicked but he loves those who pursue righteousness. Stern discipline awaits him who leaves the *path*; he who hates correction will die" (15:9-10); "The *way* of the sluggard is blocked with thorns, but the *path* of the upright is a highway" (15:19).
- Whether we have **peace even with enemies**: "When a man's *ways* are pleasing to the Lord, he makes even his enemies live at peace with him" (16:7).
- Our **stress levels**: "Her (Wisdom's) ways are pleasant *ways*, and all her *paths* are peace" (3:17).

- Our **financial condition**: "I walk in the *way* of righteousness, along the *paths* of justice, bestowing wealth on those who love me and making their treasuries full" (8:20-21).
- Whether we receive **favor from God**: "Now then, my sons, listen to me; blessed are those who *keep my ways*. Listen to my instruction and be wise; do not ignore it. Blessed is the man who listens to me, watching daily at my doors, waiting at my doorway. For whoever finds me finds life and receives favor from the Lord" (8:32-35); "The Lord detests men of perverse heart but he delights in those whose ways are blameless" (11:20); "The faithless will be fully repaid for their *ways*, and the good man rewarded for his" (14:14); "The Lord detests the *way* of the wicked but he loves those who pursue righteousness" (15:9).

By keeping our "way" in the "rutted path" marked by His Word, we enjoy so much good and avoid so much evil! By keeping on the path of righteousness, we may "miss out" on some of the short-term fun that sin can offer, but considering the long-term costs it's worth it. With promises such as less difficulty and struggle (by not complicating our lives by leaving *the path*), having peace with enemies, experiencing less stress, having financial provisions, and enjoying peace and favor from God, who needs more persuasion?

Roads Are Filled with Crossroads

Most roads have intersections—critical junctures where we choose the way to travel. Choosing left or right at some intersections will only result in minor consequences. Some will eventually lead to the same place. Some have pitfalls. Some are more difficult. Yet others are narrow, uphill paths, which are often the best ones to take in life.

Wisdom is interesting when it comes to crossroads: she is there at every turn...waiting, watching and calling us to abide by her ways: "Does not wisdom call out? Does not understanding raise her voice? On the heights along the way, where the paths meet, she takes her stand; beside the gates leading into the city, at the entrances, she cries aloud" (8:1-3). Something really profound about this passage is that it specifically mentions that wisdom is found "on the heights along the way, where the paths *meet*" and "*beside the gates* leading into the city." Wisdom is at the *crossroads*, calling into our lives when we have critical choices and decisions to make. She takes the form of God's Word, those we trust for godly counsel, a whisper or a nudge from the Holy Spirit. She often meets us at the crossroads before we choose the way we will take.

Hate the Wrong Path

The Bible doesn't use the word "hate" very often (only seventy-four times), but when it does it is typically used to describe how God feels about things that separate us from Him. Because God loves us, He despises things that separate us from Him. The writer of Psalm 119 used this strong word—hate—when describing the wrong path:

- "I gain understanding from your precepts; therefore I hate every wrong path. Your word is a lamp to my feet and a light for my path" (Psalm 119:104-105).
- "Because I love your commands more than gold, more than pure gold, and because I consider all your precepts right, I hate every wrong path" (Psalm 119:127-128).

The term "hate" is used here to describe wrong paths because they have consequences, and some have *massive consequences*. Have you ever wished you could step back in time and reverse an action? Change something you've done? Have you ever been aware of how one of your poor choices started a *chain of events* that led to a snowball effect of negative consequences? Life is a series of choices; where we end up tomorrow is a result of our choices today. Our future consists of the accumulation of our choices playing out in life. Today's planted seeds are tomorrow's fields.

This is exactly why we need grace—and thanks to God for His grace! I have experienced Christ restore me innumerable times after I've taken a wrong path. I've seen Him turn things around for the better after I've learned from my wrong choices. Wrong paths are taken by *everyone,* but the important thing is that we "get back on track" when we realize we're on the wrong road and learn from our experiences and grow.

"The path of the righteous is like the first gleam of dawn,
shining ever brighter till the full light of day"
(Proverbs 4:18).

Pillar 1: Peace-loving

The Greek term used in James 3:17 for the peace-loving pillar is *eirenikos* which means: "relating to peace, loving peace, bringing peace with one's presence; with a focus of having freedom from emotional worry and frustration."

Paul wrote thirteen books of the New Testament that are commonly referred to as the Pauline Epistles: 1 and 2 Thessalonians, 1 and 2 Corinthians, Philippians, Philemon, Galatians, Ephesians, Colossians, 1 and 2 Timothy, Titus and Romans. In every single one of these letters he included, "Grace and peace to you," or a similar greeting that held some type of peaceful wish. Even though it was a Jewish custom to extend a peaceful wish ("Shalom"), peace was continually emphasized in Paul's letters to the early church. Consider some excerpts from his writings:

- "The mind of sinful man is death, but the mind controlled by the Spirit is life and peace" (Romans 8:6).
- "If it is possible, as far as it depends on you, live at peace with everyone" (Romans 12:18).
- "Let us therefore make every effort to do what leads to peace and to mutual edification" (Romans 14:19).
- "Let the peace of Christ rule in your hearts, since as members of one body you were called to peace. And be thankful" (Colossians 3:15).

- "Now may the Lord of peace himself give you peace at all times and in every way. The Lord be with all of you" (2 Thessalonians 3:16).
- "But the fruit of the Spirit is love, joy, peace, patience, kindness, goodness, faithfulness, gentleness and self-control. Against such things there is no law. Those who belong to Christ Jesus have crucified the sinful nature with its passions and desires. Since we live by the Spirit, let us keep in step with the Spirit" (Galatians 5:22-25).
- "Rejoice in the Lord always. I will say it again: Rejoice! Let your gentleness be evident to all. The Lord is near. Do not be anxious about anything, but in everything, by prayer and petition, with thanksgiving, present your requests to God. And the peace of God, which transcends all understanding, will guard your hearts and your minds in Christ Jesus" (Philippians 4:4-7).

Paul was clear that the way to true peace was through Christ. God is the *God* of peace. Because God owns real peace, only He can provide it ("Let the peace of Christ rule in your hearts," Colossians 3:15; "Now may the Lord of peace himself give you peace at all times and in every way," 2 Thessalonians 3:16). We are filled with true peace when we are filled with the Holy Spirit (Galatians 5:22-25) and when we actively pray and release our concerns to God through Christ (Philippians 4:4-7). Only Christ can fill us with a peace that transcends our understanding and guards our hearts and our minds.

Enemies of Peace

There are some enemies to our peace. Sometimes these are found within us rather than from external circumstances. In fact, the Bible says it's often our desires that battle within us and rob peace from our lives:

What causes fights and quarrels among you? Don't they come from your desires that battle within you? You want something but don't get it. You kill and covet, but you cannot have what you want. You quarrel and fight. You do not have, because you do not ask God. When you ask, you do not receive, because you ask with wrong motives, that you may spend what you get on your pleasures (James 4:1-3).

What is the antidote for this peace-robbing thing called *desire*? Releasing it to God. People are discontent in this world because they are trying to fill up a God-shaped hole in their hearts with everything *but* God—money, thrills, music, religion, self-will and self-pride. The apostle Paul says he has learned the secret of being content in *every situation*:

> I am not saying this because I am in need, for I have learned to be content whatever the circumstances. I know what it is to be in need, and I know what it is to have plenty. I have learned the secret of *being content in any and every situation, whether well fed or hungry, whether living in plenty or in want.* I can do everything through him who gives me strength (Philippians 4:11-13).

Releasing our desires is one sure way to increase peace and decrease stress in our lives. Consider the wisdom of Thomas A. Kempis in *The Imitation of Christ* (1998, chapter 6):

> Whenever you desire anything inordinately, you immediately find that you grow dissatisfied with yourself. Those who are proud and avaricious never arrive at contentment; it is the poor and the humble in spirit who live in great peace. Anyone who is not totally dead to himself will soon find that he is tempted and overcome by piddling and frivolous things. Whoever is weak in spirit, given to the flesh, and inclined to sensual things can, but only with great difficulty, drag himself away from his earthly desires. Therefore, he is often gloomy and sad when he is trying to pull himself from them and easily gives in to anger should someone attempt to oppose him. If he has given in to his inclinations and has

yielded to his passions, he is then immediately afflicted with a guilty conscience. In no way do such yieldings help him to find the peace he seeks. It is by resisting our passions and not by being slaves to them that true peace of heart is to be found.

Consider now what Proverbs has to say about this wisdom pillar.

How to Breach a Dam
With Your Tongue

Proverbs:

- "Reckless words pierce like a sword, but the tongue of the wise brings healing" (12:18).
- "Starting a quarrel is like breaching a dam; so drop the matter before a dispute breaks out" (17:14).
- "He who loves a quarrel loves sin; he who builds a high gate invites destruction" (17:19).
- "It is to a man's honor to avoid strife, but every fool is quick to quarrel" (20:3).

Consider how fast a *split second* goes by. Think about the decisions we make and the words we say in *split seconds*. We have all made split-second decisions to *say* or *do* something we later regretted.

Law enforcement and military personnel are rigorously trained to make split- second decisions regarding the use of deadly force. They undergo lengthy and extensive classroom training and field practice exercises. *How we use our tongue* can be just as critical— and sometimes just as dangerous—as a law enforcement officer deciding whether to use deadly force! But how much training do we receive in making split-second decisions about *our speech*?

Psychologists measure human reaction time using a variety of tests. Some measure how quickly people respond after being prompted by a simple buzzer; others measure reaction time on more complex tasks such as discriminating between several letters or numbers. Our minds and bodies are so tightly connected with a complex (and *fast!*) electronic nervous system that our minds can tell our bodies to react to many simple tasks, such as jerking a steering wheel or pressing a brake pedal, in less than one-half of one second.

Have you trained yourself to make split-second decisions about whether to *speak or not* or about *what to say* if you speak? Consider the heated discussions we sometimes have with friends or loved ones. Emotions rise, our defenses escalate, and sometimes the words just slip out of our mouths like a snake striking at its victim. At that point our words have left their mark, and the injury is done.

According to James 3, our tongue is like a:

bit in the mouth of a horse—controlling the direction of the entire thousand-pound animal (verse 3).

small rudder on a ship—controlling the direction of the entire vessel (versc 4).

spark—setting fire to an entire forest (verse 5).

The tongue is such a small part of our body but can wield so much power! But why do we use it to quarrel, start dissensions or gossip? Sometimes we need to take a look *inside* to find the answer because quarreling is ultimately a *matter of the heart*. Jesus said, "The good man brings good things out of the good stored up in his heart, and the evil man brings evil things out of the evil stored up in his heart. For *out of the overflow of his heart his mouth speaks*" (Luke 6:45).

Consider the proverb: "Starting a quarrel is like breaching a dam; so drop the matter before a dispute breaks out" (17:14). Dams can hold back millions of tons of water. A dam can be breached by a very small hairline crack if it spreads across the weakest parts of the dam. As the pressure continues to have its way, the crack opens wider and wider until finally—*crash*! Learn from this verse in Proverbs—stop the quarrel before it breaks the dam. Train yourself to notice the hairline fractures—in your thinking, in the words you hear and in the words you speak. Then you will have perfected what Proverbs is conveying.

Reflect

"Don't have anything to do with foolish and stupid arguments, because you know they produce quarrels. And the Lord's servant must not quarrel; instead, he must be kind to everyone, able to teach, not resentful. Those who oppose him he must gently instruct, in the hope that God will grant them repentance leading them to a knowledge of the truth, and that they will come to their senses and escape from the trap of the devil, who has taken them captive to do his will" (2 Timothy 2:23-26).

Be Quick to Listen and Slow to Speak

Proverbs:

- "When words are many, sin is not absent, but he who holds his tongue is wise" (10:19).
- "A man finds joy in giving an apt reply—and how good is a timely word!" (15:23).
- "A wise man's heart guides his mouth, and his lips promote instruction" (16:23).
- "A man of knowledge uses words with restraint, and a man of understanding is even-tempered. Even a fool is thought wise if he keeps silent, and discerning if he holds his tongue" (17:27-28).
- "He who answers before listening—that is his folly and his shame" (18:13).
- "A word aptly spoken is like apples of gold in settings of silver" (25:11).
- "Do you see a man who speaks in haste? There is more hope for a fool than for him" (29:20).

There is a time for flowing, loving and carefree conversation. There is also a time for short and pointed (but loving) words (for example, Proverbs 25:11 above). Communication when emotions are running high is sometimes like a tennis match. Inexperienced tennis players will often "go for the kill shot" too early during a rally and end up hitting the ball out of bounds. Experienced athletes, however, will "play the round" until it's finished—only taking the kill shot *when it's there to be taken.* The key difference when applying this to engaging in wise conversation is that you're trying to win a point *for* a person, not *against* them ("Do not let any unwholesome talk come out of your mouths, but only what is helpful for building others up according to their needs, that it may benefit those who listen," Ephesians 4:29).

The late Dr. Walter Martin was known as the original "Bible Answer Man." Dr. Martin had a steel-trap mind for knowledge and facts and had enough verbal fluency to win a debate with just about anyone. As the host of a radio program for several years, he would take questions from callers who would dream up questions loaded with complexities and fire them at Dr. Martin, who had little time to prepare. On one of these calls I thought the caller (John) had pinned him down with a question that was seemingly unanswerable. I thought Dr. Martin was stuck.

There was a long stretch of silence on the airwaves as he paused for a time. And then a very short, calm and loving answer came back: "John, what are you going to do with Jesus Christ, and are you content that what you believe about *Him* is going to prepare you for eternity?" After disarming him and digging deeper into where this man was *personally* rather than *theologically,* he later led him to Christ over the phone. Instead of getting tied up in a theological pretzel, Dr. Martin seemed to sense that this man didn't even really want an answer but was just calling out of his own personal frustration on what to do with the big question we all must answer (*Who really is Jesus Christ?*). Rather than entering into "biblical sword play," Dr. Martin gracefully went directly to the very heart of the issue. Clearly, a word aptly spoken is like "apples of gold in settings of silver" (Proverbs 25:11).

Sometimes I give expert testimony in court cases. The court reporter records every word I speak. After I verbally offer an opinion on a certain issue, there's no taking it back. It's like writing a book in "real time" using a permanent marker. This same concept can be true in life. Trying to take back our words is like trying to unscramble eggs. That's why God gave us two ears and one mouth—so we will listen twice as much as we speak.

So much peace is brought into our lives—or taken from our lives—by our daily choices to truly listen before we speak. True listening involves your whole person: heart, mind, body and soul. Communication is perfected only when our speaking also involves each of these elements. We apply our hearts by identifying with the speaker and having empathy. We use our minds by carefully working through what they are saying. Our bodies are, of course, the physical channel for listening—the gateway through which all communication is received. Directing our focus on the speaker by being attentive and making eye contact are basic communication skills, but how many of us still need help in this area? Listening with our spirits is the most difficult. It takes years of practice to become skilled in this area, but it's the most important part of listening. This skill is shown by those who can apply the first three skills—listening with their hearts, minds and bodies—and who can go one step further by hearing from God, sensing His best for a situation and then advising accordingly. The one who applies this skill has refined the art of godly listening.

Reflect

"My dear brothers, take note of this: Everyone should be quick to listen, slow to speak and slow to become angry, for man's anger does not bring about the righteous life that God desires. Therefore, get rid of all moral filth and the evil that is so prevalent and humbly accept the word planted in you, which can save you" (James 1:19-21).

Preach the gospel at all times. Use words if necessary.
—Saint Francis of Assisi.

The Poison of Gossip

Proverbs:

- "A gossip betrays a confidence, but a trustworthy man keeps a secret" (11:13).
- "A perverse man stirs up dissension, and a gossip separates close friends" (16:28).
- "A fool's mouth is his undoing, and his lips are a snare to his soul. The words of a gossip are like choice morsels; they go down to a man's inmost parts" (18:7-8, see also 26:22).
- "A gossip betrays a confidence; so avoid a man who talks too much" (20:19).
- "Without wood a fire goes out; without gossip a quarrel dies down" (26:20).

Few things can disrupt a peaceful life more than gossip. Indeed, everyone reading this book has doubtless been on both the sending and receiving end of gossip and has felt the tension created by it. Gossip can impact your inner peace in ways you are aware of and even in ways you are *unaware* of because it can become lodged in your inner heart and subtly disrupt your state of being.

We've all experienced the pain that comes from *being gossiped about*. Yet despite this we still continue because it's difficult not to gossip. Sometimes our mouths work faster than our minds and our good sense, and before we know it the words are out. With gossip having such potential for making massive and lasting negative impact, it will be helpful to understand just what gossip is, the specific impact it has on our lives and how we can disarm it effectively.

What is Gossip?

The biblical terms used for "gossip" in the passages above vary in definition but can be translated to include these modern-day meanings:

- Slandering or libeling (in fact, some modern transla-tions use the term "slanderer" rather than "gossip" in the passages above)
- Grumbling and complaining
- Spreading "hearsay"
- Telling "tall tales" or exaggerating
- Breaking a confidence

However defined, gossip is the means for spreading negativity and dissension in the church, workplace, home and other social networks. A dangerous characteristic of gossip is that it tends to decrease in accuracy the more it is spread. Individuals who partici-pate in gossiping often do so because they believe it increases their importance and builds their self-esteem (by being "in the know" compared to others).

There is a fine line between "information sharing" and gossip, but there are ways to tell the difference between the two. First, ask yourself: Would you share this information if the person it's about was present? Second, consider whether you would want someone sharing this type of information about you. And, third, question your motivation behind wanting to share the information. Why do you *really* want to share this information? Is it to benefit or build up the listener? Ephesians 4:29 admonishes: "Do not let any unwhole-some talk come out of your mouths, but only what is helpful for building others up according to *their needs*, that it may benefit those who listen." How much better would our relationships be if we were mostly concerned with building up and strengthening others according to their needs, rather than our own?

What are the Consequences of Gossip?

According to the passages above, gossip betrays a confidence, stirs up dissension, separates close friends, has a negative and lasting impact (is "swallowed up" as described in 18:7-8) and, most sadly, can offend a relative or friend and make them "more unyielding than a fortified city." Commenting on the "innermost being" mentioned in Proverbs 18:7-8, Waltke (2005, p. 74) describes this as representing "the deepest and most complete stratum of a person's psyche" and explains that because slander so thoroughly penetrates a person's thoughts and emotions, it remains indelibly imprinted in our minds and hearts. If we are to experience peace and offer it to others we need to separate ourselves from gossip.

How to Deal with Gossip

Because gossip is highly contagious and the human heart has little resistance to it, the most effective cure (as hinted by the verses above) is to *quarantine* it by not repeating it to others (see Proverbs 16:28, 17:9, 26:20). Another effective method is to encourage the gossiper to go directly to the person they are gossiping about and deal directly with them about the issue. Another effective technique is to tell them you would rather not hear it. Still another way is simply to avoid the gossipers (Proverbs 20:19).

If you are in a position of leadership, providing regular and consistent communication with those under you is one way to effectively combat gossip. This minimizes the influence gossiping individuals have over others because everyone shares in the same set of facts. Not participating in spreading gossip and rumors also sets a good example for others to model.

Reflect

So live that you wouldn't be ashamed to sell the family parrot
to the town gossip.
—Will Rogers

Whoever gossips to you will gossip about you.
—Spanish Proverb

Taking the High Road

Proverbs:

- "A fool shows his annoyance at once, but a prudent man overlooks an insult" (12:16).
- "A man's wisdom gives him patience; it is to his glory to overlook an offense" (19:11).
- "Do not answer a fool according to his folly, or you will be like him yourself. Answer a fool according to his folly, or he will be wise in his own eyes" (26:4-5).

- **"A fool gives full vent to his anger, but a wise man keeps himself under control" (29:11).**

As a young man, I worked for my father in the family business. He owned the building our company occupied, and a few of our office suites were rented out to other businesses. One winter we were remodeling the building, and the heating system had to be shut down for a few days. During the dead of winter this made some of the tenants rightfully angry. One early morning I went to work, and before I could grab my first cup of coffee one of the tenants came to our office and read me the "riot act." She really let me have it. She was cold, her staff was cold, and she thought it was about time the heating system was turned back on. At the top of her voice and with her finger wagging in my face, she exclaimed, "You go tell your daddy to get the heater fixed, or we're moving out next week and not paying rent!" As a young man in my twenties, I could think of no worse insult than another adult telling me to "go tell my daddy" to fix a problem. Luckily, before I could say anything in response to her rage, she stormed out the door.

When my dad came in the office an hour later, I poured out my frustration: "You wouldn't believe how disrespectful she was to me! She told me to 'go tell my daddy!' Can you believe it? I would just prefer it if she *did* move out!" My dad let me vent for a while, but then he asked me to do the impossible: "Dan, I know that what she said to you was disrespectful, and it probably made you very angry—and rightfully so, but I'd like you to go and see her before you go home today, apologize to her that the heating system has not been working and tell her we'll be sure to get it fixed as soon as possible." "What?" I shrugged. "Are you out of your mind? She treated me like an eight-year-old—telling me to go and 'get my daddy' while stuffing her finger in my face—and you want *me* to go apologize to *her*? Give me a break!"

He then explained that sometimes in life you can be "right" but also be "dead right." In other words, yes, she offended me and I didn't deserve her condescending speech, but for me to go and demand an apology from her, a person who had been paying rent for "good service" we were not providing, was not a "strategically beneficial" move. No matter how unpleasant her message was, it was a valid message nonetheless and one we needed to act upon to be diligent landlords.

From my dad's vantage point our company needed their rent money, and she was right: since she was one of our tenants, it was our job to provide her with top-quality service; allowing her heating system to go for so many days without working (especially in the winter) was unacceptable. We needed to get it fixed—and fast. She never did apologize to me for the way she acted, but that was okay because I grew immeasurably as a result of going through that experience.

Proverbs 26:4-5 provides an apparently contradictory set of proverbial pairs (proverbs that are topically similar or appear close together in the text). Verse 4 says we should *not* answer a fool according to his folly, or we will be just like the fool himself. Verse 5, however, says if we *don't* answer a fool according to his folly, he will be wise in his own eyes. This seems like quite the conundrum—we're told the wise should answer a fool and also instructed not to answer the fool. Fortunately there is a reason for this apparent contradiction. Consider the following truths that are revealed only by the combination of both verses:

- No matter what the circumstances involve, the fool must be kept in his place.
- The folly, but not necessarily the fool bringing the folly, must be answered by the wise.
- There is no routine approach for handling a fool.
- Discernment on the part of the wise is needed in all circumstances.
- Entering into dialogue with a fool is both an *obligation and a challenge* for the wise (Murphy, 1998, p. 203).

Sometimes a fool needs to be put in his place, while in other circumstances even answering a fool is not a wise choice. For example, when Nehemiah set out to rebuild the walls of Jerusalem, he was continually harassed and falsely accused by Sanballat, the

leader of a group who opposed Nehemiah's work. After toler-
ating the lies and accusations for weeks, Nehemiah eventually
responded in writing to Sanballat—dispelling all truth in his falsi-
ties (Nehemiah 6:5-8).

Let's be honest—it is both easy and self-satisfying to take the
"low road" when being challenged by a fool. But the way of peace
and wisdom is to use discretion and weigh the stakes of the situation, while also discerning the motivations behind your desired
actions. If the stakes are small and self-pride is the motivation,
staying silent and turning the other cheek is usually the best course
of action. If, however, the stakes involve your character and cred-
ibility, and truth and peace are your motivations, then speaking up
in a tone and manner that honor God and your listeners is the best
way to respond.

Reflect

"Do not be quickly provoked in your spirit, for anger resides
in the lap of fools" (Ecclesiastes 7:9).

"My dear brothers, take note of this: Everyone should be
quick to listen, slow to speak and slow to become angry, for
man's anger does not bring about the righteous life that God
desires" (James 1:19-20).

"You have heard that it was said, 'Eye for eye, and tooth for
tooth.' But I tell you, do not resist an evil person. If someone
strikes you on the right cheek, turn to him the other also.
And if someone wants to sue you and take your tunic, let
him have your cloak as well. If someone forces you to go
one mile, go with him two miles. Give to the one who asks
you, and do not turn away from the one who wants to borrow
from you" (Matthew 5:38-42).

"And the Lord's servant must not quarrel; instead, he must
be kind to everyone, able to teach, not resentful. Those who
oppose him he must gently instruct, in the hope that God will

grant them repentance leading them to a knowledge of the truth" (2 Timothy 2:24-26).

"Blessed are the meek, for they will inherit the earth"
(Matthew 5:5).

Patience

- "A patient man has great understanding, but a quick-tempered man displays folly" (14:29).
- "A hot-tempered man stirs up dissension, but a patient man calms a quarrel" (15:18).
- "Better a patient man than a warrior, a man who controls his temper than one who takes a city" (16:32).
- "A man's wisdom gives him patience; it is to his glory to overlook an offense" (19:11).
- "Through patience a ruler can be persuaded, and a gentle tongue can break a bone" (25:15).

According to the verses above, patience (or the lack thereof) can have a powerful impact on many areas of our lives. Patience can create a situation of mutual understanding to help build consensus, avoid foolishness and folly, turn away and disarm anger brought by others, contain and subdue temper and anger, avoid dissension, calm a quarrel, help overlook an offense and even sway rulers and leaders.

So how do we gain this priceless virtue of "patience?" Patience is grown, not acquired. It is slowly cultivated in our lives, not micro-waved. Sure, God can (and does) give us patience and wisdom as a fruit of His Spirit. But God grows our patience by *passing us through difficult circumstances*. Consider the following Scripture verses:

- "For our light and momentary troubles are *achieving for us* an eternal glory that far outweighs them all. So we fix our eyes not on what is seen, but on what is unseen. For what is seen is temporary, but what is unseen is eternal" (2 Corinthians 4:17-18).
- "Not only so, but we also rejoice in our sufferings, because we know that suffering produces perseverance; perseverance, character; and character, hope. And hope does not disappoint us, because God has poured out his love into our hearts by the Holy Spirit, whom he has given us" (Romans 5:3-5).
- "Consider it pure joy, my brothers, whenever you face trials of many kinds, because you know that the testing of your faith develops perseverance. Perseverance must finish its work so that you may be mature and complete, not lacking anything" (James 1:2-4).

These passages deliver two important truths. First, God wants us to grow—especially in areas of perseverance and endurance (that is, patience). Second, He gracefully allows us to endure trials and tribulations that *grow* these assets in our lives. They are often His tools that shape and refine these timeless virtues in our character. And as we actually see the incredible benefits of patience that grow from the "light and momentary troubles" (2 Corinthians 4:17) we will be truly grateful.

In Hebrew the term "patience" literally means "to have a long nose" (with "nose" representing the face or some part of the face). "Hot of nose" signifies anger, "long of nose" signifies patience, and "high of nose" signifies arrogance. As funny as this may sound, hot-tempered people tend to "flare their nostrils" when they get angry. Refraining from this behavior means to exhibit patience (to have a long nose and not a flared one!). So how do we grow long noses and not flaring ones? There are two primary ways. First, we pray. Second, we endure *through* the situation God has allowed in our lives. Sometimes this requires making a deliberate "mind over matter" decision to choose patience over emotions. Here are a few examples of how to practically apply these concepts.

In the days before e-mail, office professionals often communicated using handwritten memos in office "in-boxes." Sometimes these notes were of the "you should have done better on this project" variety. When it came to making notes of this nature, my dad would write a note to a staff member but let it "season" for one day in the top, right-hand drawer of his desk. If he came in the next day and still felt like the note should be delivered as written, he would go ahead and deliver it. But if he thought he should "tone it down a little" first, he would. Most of the time he would rewrite the note or not deliver it at all and end up taking the "high road" with the staff member by just talking it over with them.

This is a practical demonstration of what these verses in Proverbs are saying. It is a good example of how to use your brain to control your emotions. For some of us it might involve leaving the situation. For others it might be counting to ten before responding. Patience is a "muscle" in a sense—the more we use it, the stronger it gets.

The Lord recently gave me an opportunity to "grow more patience." I was on an errand with my daughter Alyssa and son Matthew to buy some bookshelves for the office. After having no luck at the first store, we raced off to the big "mega-furniture" store. This brand new store wasn't even on the map, but some of my friends had been there recently and gave me general directions. I'm usually quite picky about making sure I understand the directions before I venture out, but on this occasion this was the best information I had.

So began the wild goose chase. The more we drove, the more lost we became. My daughter started becoming car sick because of my erratic driving. I made a second call to confirm the directions but ended up becoming more lost. Soon another twenty minutes was wasted, and more impatience ensued. After about forty-five minutes of nonsense I was tempted to go home defeated and confused. I didn't have the patience that day to deal with the situation, but I persevered and called yet another person, who again only generally knew where the store was but sounded confident. There went another fifteen minutes.

I finally called the store. After *patiently* waiting on hold for an operator (another ten minutes), I got directions (which were exactly the same as those given by my friends, making me feel even worse!) that pinned down the store location. When all was said and done, we had spent over an hour being lost.

Rather than wasting the experience, I traded it for an additional ounce of patience. I made a *decision of will* to use the situation as an opportunity to grow more patience. It certainly wasn't how I felt like responding, but the choice to respond to the challenge with patience was rewarded with blessings. I'm sure our heavenly Father has us endure challenging situations so we can improve our character and temperament. You see—that's the only way patience can grow— when we have to apply it or, better yet, when we *choose* to apply it.

Blessings always seem to come after applying patience. Even if we don't receive the reward immediately, we will in the long run because we traded the stressful situation for a heap of character and wisdom that will help us through similar situations that later may arise in our lives.

Reflect

"If a ruler's anger rises against you, do not leave your post; calmness can lay great errors to rest" (Ecclesiastes 10:4).

"Do not be quickly provoked in your spirit, for anger resides in the lap of fools" (Ecclesiastes 7:9).

"My dear brothers, take note of this: Everyone should be quick to listen, slow to speak and slow to become angry, for man's anger does not bring about the righteous life that God desires. Therefore, get rid of all moral filth and the evil that is so prevalent and humbly accept the word planted in you, which can save you" (James 1:19-21).

Pillar 2: Considerate

The Greek term used in James 3:17 for the considerate wisdom pillar is *epieikes*, which means "seemingly, suitable, equitable, fair, mild and gentle." This term is used only five times in the New Testament. In two of these instances it is translated in the NIV Bible as *gentle* or *gentleness* and three times as *considerate*:

- "Rejoice in the Lord always. I will say it again: Rejoice! Let your *gentleness* be evident to all. The Lord is near" (Philippians 4:4-5).
- "Here is a trustworthy saying: If anyone sets his heart on being an overseer, he desires a noble task. Now the overseer must be above reproach, the husband of but one wife, temperate, self-controlled, respectable, hospitable, able to teach, not given to drunkenness, not violent but *gentle*, not quarrelsome, not a lover of money" (1Timothy 3:1-3).
- "Remind the people to be subject to rulers and authorities, to be obedient, to be ready to do whatever is good, to slander no one, to be peaceable and *considerate*, and to show true humility toward all men" (Titus 3:1-2).
- "But the wisdom that comes from heaven is first of all pure; then peace-loving, *considerate*, submissive, full of mercy and good fruit, impartial and sincere" (James 3:17).
- "Slaves, submit yourselves to your masters with all respect, not only to those who are good and *considerate*, but also to those who are harsh. For it is commendable if a man

bears up under the pain of unjust suffering because he is conscious of God" (1 Peter 2:18-19).

Acting out this Christ-like trait of "being considerate and gentle" involves a whole lot more than just opening a door for someone, although it certainly includes such actions. Being considerate really comes down to being *others-focused*, which requires two key practices: *denying yourself* (a submissive, passive act) and *actively seeking the good of others* (action-oriented). Each of these will be explored now as we look into what Proverbs has to say about this wisdom pillar.

How to *Really* Accept Others

Proverbs:

- "A friend loves at all times, and a brother is born for adversity" (17:17).
- "A man of many companions may come to ruin, but there is a friend who sticks closer than a brother" (18:24).

Do you pay attention to the needs of others around you? Jesus did. In fact, it seems like the only time He spent away from others was to pray and gain strength so He could serve others even more. Being considerate of others means being *others-focused*. And being others-focused is what Christian love demands: "Each of you should look not only to your own interests, but also to the interests of others" (Philippians 2:4).

But what about dealing with really difficult people? Especially if their personality defects are perfectly aligned with our irritation points? Fifteenth-century Christian author, Thomas A. Kempis, offers advice for such challenges (paraphrased from the original writing):

Strive to always be patient with the faults and imperfections of others, for you have many faults and imperfections of your own that require the patience of others. If you are not able to make yourself into the person you would like to be, then how can you expect to mold another in conformity to your will?

Why do we become so frustrated when dealing with the imperfections of others if we cannot even change our own? Paul's words in Ephesians 4:2-3 encourage us to *bear with each other* and to *make every effort to keep unity*: "Be completely humble and gentle; be patient, bearing with one another in love. Make every effort to keep the unity of the Spirit through the bond of peace."

As a young man, I worked in a receiving warehouse for a large retailer. Shipments would come in by truck around 6:00 a.m., and our crew of twenty workers had to unload truckload after truckload of inventory. Our supervisor's role was to "motivate" our crew to get the job done as quickly as possible, and he would use every technique in the book to do so. The only problem was that his motivation methods tended to be manipulative, condescending and sometimes just plain rude.

I imagine that all of the workers in our crew developed their own ways of coping with this individual. After struggling to find my own, I finally found one that helped me survive his barrage of control tactics. I remember using an acronym to remember my technique and be ready to buffer myself against his harshness in a moment's notice. It was U-A-L, which stood for **U**nderstand, **A**ccept and **L**ove. I thought, "If I can really try to Understand this man's background — how he was raised, what his childhood must have been like — then I will be able to Accept him and ultimately be able to Love him.

It wasn't until years later that I understood the biblical model is completely reverse. The biblical model is to love and accept others *first*, as God loves and accepts us. The *understanding* part is actually optional as far as the Lord is concerned — you might never understand someone or their actions, but we are still commanded to love them.

Love

- "A new command I give you: Love one another. As I have loved you, so you must love one another. By this all men will know that you are my disciples, if you love one another" (John 13:34-35).

- "Dear friends, let us love one another, for love comes from God. Everyone who loves has been born of God and knows God" (1 John 4:7).

Accept

- "If you love those who love you, what reward will you get? Are not even the tax collectors doing that? And if you greet only your brothers, what are you doing more than others? Do not even pagans do that? Be perfect, therefore, as your heavenly Father is perfect" (Matthew 5:46-48).

- "Bear with each other and forgive whatever grievances you may have against one another. Forgive as the Lord forgave you. And over all these virtues put on love, which binds them all together in perfect unity" (Colossians 3:13-14).

Understand

- "Praise be to the God and Father of our Lord Jesus Christ, the Father of compassion and the God of all comfort, who comforts us in all our troubles, so that we can comfort those in any trouble with the comfort we ourselves have received from God. For just as the sufferings of Christ flow over into our lives, so also through Christ our comfort overflows" (2 Corinthians 1:3-5).

Our actions sometimes upset God. Do you believe He is patient with you during these times? Yes, of course He is. How should this impact the way we treat others? We all have personality quirks that irritate others. May we be more patient in dealing with others and practice the command to "love at all times" as Proverbs 17:17 suggests.

Reflect

We can do no great things, only small things with great love.
—Mother Teresa

There is nothing as strong as true gentleness and nothing as gentle as true strength.
—Peter Briggs

Exchanging Money for Character

Proverbs:

- "One man gives freely, yet gains even more; another withholds unduly, but comes to poverty. A generous man will prosper; he who refreshes others will himself be refreshed. People curse the man who hoards grain, but blessing crowns him who is willing to sell" (11:24-26).

M y father, Dick Biddle, grew up with a friend named Russell Avery. Russell's father, R. Stanton Avery, was the founder of the Avery label company, which is now one of the leading manufacturers of adhesive labels with annual sales exceeding $5.5 billion. My dad tells a story of doing weekend chores for Mr. Avery to earn money for his first car:

"Five dollars a cord," Mr. Avery offered generously. "For every cord of wood you chop I'll give you five bucks." Five dollars was a lot of money to a young man in the 1950s, and despite feeling that Mr. Avery was being overly generous my dad started tackling the chore. As he began splitting the wood, Mr. Avery pointed to a stack of extra hickory axe handles leaning against the wood shed and said: "If you break an axe handle, there are a dozen extra over there. You just take the axe head off the broken handle and slide it onto the new handle, and you're good to go. By the way, a cord of split wood is measured eight feet by four feet by four feet—no more and no less. And you should be able to chop two or three cords in a day if you stay focused. I will pay you when I return tonight."

So my father began. After only a half hour of chopping—crack! The first nicely hewn axe handle snapped across the top of the log as he missed. Hickory axe handles were the most expensive type because they were usually strong enough to withstand a few misses, but none seemed strong enough to survive the impact of a complete miss by this ambitious teenager.

After two hours of chopping he had gone through three axe handles. Feeling badly, he took a break and thought about sharpening his aim and slowing down a little. But knowing he still had a lot of wood to chop to reach his goal of two or three cords, he continued. After another two hours he was down to only six axe handles, with the other six splintered and stacked.

After six hours my dad had two cords neatly stacked, but only four axe handles remained. At the end of the long day he finally had three cords stacked, and only two axe handles remained. The other ten were shattered and heaped together in a mound.

Finally Mr. Avery returned. "How'd your day go, Dick?" he asked. My dad felt too shameful about the ten broken axe handles to say anything about his day's performance. Eyeing the three neatly stacked cords of wood, Mr. Avery said proudly: "I didn't think you'd get three finished—good job!" "Yeah," my dad said, "but I feel so terrible. I broke nearly *all* of your hickory axe handles, Mr. Avery. How much do they cost?" Mr. Avery replied gently, "Oh, they're only about three bucks a piece, but don't worry about it." The cogs in Dad's mind turned quickly as he cranked out the math: *Three dollars a piece times ten is thirty dollars,* he thought to himself. *Mr. Avery is about to pay me fifteen dollars for the three cords of wood, but my sloppy chopping cost him thirty dollars in broken axe handles.*

Mr. Avery expressed gratitude to my father for a job well done and said, "I'll have another dozen axe handles ready for you next weekend if you'd like to earn some more money." Baffled, my father took his fifteen dollars and sore hands home to rest.

While it probably took several years to sink in, my dad grew to understand he hadn't gone to Mr. Avery's house to chop wood that day. He had gone to Mr. Avery's house so he could learn a lesson in work ethic and generosity. By offering his time and money, Mr. Avery's generosity installed forty-five *priceless* dollars of character into my dad, who in turn passed along similar lessons to hundreds of others throughout his life.

Sometimes we need to spend our worldly wealth on character development. It's our obligation and privilege to allow others to break our "axe handles" so they can grow personally. The cost of this process should be factored into the cost of each split log. Don't get upset at a child who breaks a thirty-dollar vase in a store; rather translate the experience into a thirty-dollar lesson in carefulness. Money is a resource and a tool—it's not one of *your assets.* God could cause your wealth to increase or shrink in a single day. Do you have much? Then use your wealth to help others to grow and discover their talent and opportunities. As the Master said, "I tell you, use worldly wealth to gain friends for yourselves, so that when it is gone, you will be welcomed into eternal dwellings" (Luke 16:9).

So Why Be Generous?

- "All day long he craves for more, but the righteous give without sparing" (21:26).
- "Do not eat the food of a stingy man, do not crave his delicacies; for he is the kind of man who is always thinking about the cost. 'Eat and drink,' he says to you, but his heart is not with you. You will vomit up the little you have eaten and will have wasted your compliments" (23:6-8).
- "A stingy man is eager to get rich and is unaware that poverty awaits him" (28:22).
- "A greedy man stirs up dissension, but he who trusts in the Lord will prosper" (28:25).
- "He who gives to the poor will lack nothing, but he who closes his eyes to them receives many curses" (28:27).

Biblical principles surrounding finances are often the opposite of what the world teaches. Consider the contrasts between worldly and biblical views about money.

The World Teaches	The Bible Teaches	Scripture Reference
The one who dies with the most toys wins	The one who gives away the most wins	Proverbs 11:24-26
Use riches to gain friends	Use riches to save souls and share with those in need	Luke 16:9, Acts 4:32
Use money to enjoy the present to its fullest	Using money (a temporary resource) properly will gain permanent blessing in eternity	Luke 12:21, Matthew 6:19-21
Wealth = Security	Christ = Security	1 Timothy 6:17-19, Matthew 6:19-21
Receive before you give	Give to receive	2 Corinthians 9:6-11, Luke 6:38
Keep money and enjoy it for yourself	Give money to God and others to enjoy a truly fulfilled life	Proverbs 3:9-10, 11:25-26
Gaining more and more wealth is the most important thing in life	Being a good steward of the resources you are entrusted with is most important	Luke 9:25

Greed is *self*-focused, generosity is *others*-focused, and being others-focused is what being considerate is all about. God wants us to be generous for several reasons.

Being generous:

- Teaches us that money is not everything it is cracked up to be and that it is better to give it away willingly and joyfully while we are alive than to simply lose it all reluctantly when we pass away. As Christ commands, "But seek first his kingdom and his righteousness, and all these things will be given to you as well" (Matthew 6:33). No one has ever seen a hearse towing a U-haul.
- Passes blessing from this temporary life into the coming life, which is eternal: "Do not store up for yourselves treasures on earth, where moth and rust destroy, and where thieves break in and steal. But store up for yourselves treasures in heaven, where moth and rust do not destroy, and where thieves do not break in and steal. For where your treasure is, there your heart will be also" (Matthew 6:19-21).
- Provides for the needs of others: "All the believers were one in heart and mind. No one claimed that any of his possessions was his own, but they shared everything they had. With great power the apostles continued to testify to the resurrection of the Lord Jesus, and much grace was upon them all. There were no needy persons among them. For from time to time those who owned lands or houses sold them, brought the money from the sales and put it at the apostles' feet, and it was distributed to anyone as he had need" (Acts 5:32-35).

Even those of us who are "just getting by" in America are vastly more wealthy than most of the world. Do you have *any* discretionary money? *Any* income that is above your baseline needs (your house payment, car and other living expenses)? If so, God will hold you responsible for how you use the overage. Discerning *when* to give (there is a right time for everything, and being sensitive to God's prompting is key), *why* to give (based on the true *needs* of others, not their *wants*) and *how much* to give is the art of generous giving we all need to learn.

Whenever you have overage in your life, being a trustworthy and generous steward will be one of your missions. There is nothing wrong with spending some of our discretionary money for personal enjoyment. After all, part of what keeps us motivated is being able to enjoy some of the "fruit" of our labor. But striking the delicate balance between self-indulgence and luxury is a challenge for all of us—one we need God to lead us through.

Reflect

To live content with small means; to seek elegance rather than luxury, and refinement rather than fashion; to be worthy, not respectable, and wealthy, not rich; to listen to stars and birds, babes and sages, with open heart; to study hard; to think quietly, act frankly, talk gently, await occasions, hurry never; in a word, to let the spiritual, unbidden and unconscious, grow up through the common—this is my symphony.
—William Henry Channing

"From everyone who has been given much, much will be demanded; and from the one who has been entrusted with much, much more will be asked" (Luke 12:48).

"Remember this: Whoever sows sparingly will also reap sparingly, and whoever sows generously will also reap generously. Each man should give what he has decided in his heart to give, not reluctantly or under compulsion, for God loves a cheerful giver. And God is able to make all grace abound to you, so that in all things at all times, having all that you need, you will abound in every good work. As it is written: 'He has scattered abroad his gifts to the poor; his righteousness endures forever.' Now he who supplies seed to the sower and bread for food will also supply and increase your store of seed and will enlarge the harvest of your righteousness. You will be made rich in every way so that you can be generous on every occasion, and through us your generosity will result in thanksgiving to God" (2 Corinthians 9:6-11).

"Give, and it will be given to you. A good measure, pressed down, shaken together and running over, will be poured into your lap. For with the measure you use, it will be measured to you" (Luke 6:38).

"Command those who are rich in this present world not to be arrogant nor to put their hope in wealth, which is so uncertain, but to put their hope in God, who richly provides us with everything for our enjoyment. Command them to do good, to be rich in good deeds, and to be generous and willing to share. In this way they will lay up treasure for themselves as a firm foundation for the coming age, so that they may take hold of the life that is truly life" (1 Timothy 6:17-19).

A Strategy for Real Victory

Proverbs:

- "The proverbs of Solomon son of David, king of Israel: for attaining wisdom and discipline; for understanding words of insight; for acquiring a disciplined and prudent life, doing what is right and just and fair; for giving prudence to the simple, knowledge and discretion to the young—let the wise listen and add to their learning, and let the discerning get guidance—for understanding proverbs and parables, the sayings and riddles of the wise" (1:1-6).
- "If a king judges the poor with fairness, his throne will always be secure" (29:14).
- "Even a child is known by his actions, by whether his conduct is pure and right" (20:11).

It was an early Saturday morning. My oldest daughter, Makaela, and I were dressed in our soccer uniforms as "player" and "coach," and we sat on a cold playground curb waiting for the opposing team to show up for our scheduled game. One by one they arrived with visibly nervous faces to play our so-far undefeated team. Within the first twenty seconds of the game we scored a first goal. Five minutes later another goal was scored. Twenty minutes into the first half, the ball had only been on our half of the field for about one minute, and we had posted our third goal.

At halftime I pulled most of our goal-scoring forwards either out of the game or assigned them positions in the backfield—positions in which they had little practice. Needing to find other ways to slightly handicap our team so as to not make a mockery of the other team (already looking demoralized), I assigned my daughter as goal-keeper, a position she had never before played in a game. Reluctant at first, she suited up for the position. Despite all these attempts to purposefully hamper our team, our winning trend continued as our regular goal-keeper (now playing center forward), knocked in two goals at the start of the second half. Now the score was 5-0. Soon it was 6-0; then 7-0.

In a desperate attempt to avoid a shut-out the other team played all eleven players as goal-scoring forwards in the last five minutes of the game. Every single one of their players lined up on the half-field line for their kickoff then began their march down the field to score on my daughter. Never before seeing an entire team playing only offensive positions, my daughter's eyes grew as big as giant tennis balls. It turned into a shooting gallery. My daughter ended up stopping two goals and letting one in—making for a final score of 8-1.

After the game their coach and all three referees ganged up on me to ask me how I could allow my players to completely stomp the other team. All of their girls were disheartened, and their goal-keeper was in tears. What more was I supposed to do? Just throw the game? Take players off the field? Because our team plays in a recreational (rather than a competitive) league, the unspoken "spirit of the game" is to focus on the sportsmanship and skill of the game, rather than going for such a victory run. After explaining everything I had done to handicap our team (which was everything but playing with a six-person team or scoring goals on ourselves!), their coach calmed down.

One of our primary purposes during games is to let the girls have fun, be competitive and play their best. But another objective, and the one that was tested that day, was to be fair, balanced and equitable. This is where this story connects with the wisdom pillar of being "considerate." The Greek term for *considerate* used in James 3:17 is *epieikes*, which means equitable, fair, mild and gentle. Notice this definition includes *equitable and fair*. King Solomon insists that the

Proverbs are given for doing what is right and just and fair. Abiding by fairness—especially with those weaker or less fortunate than us—can result in our "thrones" (our leadership post or our family estate) *always being secure* (Proverbs 29:14). And, if "even a child is known by his actions, by whether his conduct is pure and right" (Proverbs 20:11), how much more so will our actions be known in our own lives? Do we find ways to set aside personal glory for the growth and recognition of others? True leaders take all the blame yet give away all the credit.

Loving When You Are
Too Tired to Love

Proverbs:

- "A kindhearted woman gains respect, but ruthless men gain only wealth" (11:16).
- "A generous man will prosper; he who refreshes others will himself be refreshed" (11:25).
- "A friend loves at all times, and a brother is born for adversity" (17:17).
- "She sets about her work vigorously; her arms are strong for her tasks" (31:17).

It's easy to love and care for people when you feel energized and enthusiastic. But what about when you feel too tired to love? When you've spent all your energy and enthusiasm and you're *just plain done*? That's when your *will* comes in and you make the *decision* to apply your will over your feelings and give a little. That's when being considerate counts. Truly this is a life skill that every student, parent and professional desperately needs.

Perhaps no occupation in life demands this skill more than being a mother. I returned from a business trip recently to find my wife suffering from a cold, an ear infection, a sore tailbone from a soccer accident and a pinched nerve in her back. None of these ailments stopped her from meeting the needs of our family.

Her strong will to be considerate and meet the needs of her family overcame her physical limitations. She had good reason to lie down and recuperate; but the needs of our family demanded her effort, and she pushed through the difficulties. This is why I lovingly sometimes call her "Proverbs 31" (a chapter in Proverbs dedicated to describing a godly woman).

Consider what the following passages have to say about serving and putting the needs of others above your own:

- "Do everything without complaining or arguing, so that you may become blameless and pure, children of God without fault in a crooked and depraved generation, in which you shine like stars in the universe as you hold out the word of life—in order that I may boast on the day of Christ that I did not run or labor for nothing" (Philippians 2:14-17).
- "Carry each other's burdens, and in this way you will fulfill the law of Christ" (Galatians 6:2).
- "We who are strong ought to bear with the failings of the weak and not to please ourselves. Each of us should please his neighbor for his good, to build him up. For even Christ did not please himself" (Romans 15:1-3).
- "And we urge you, brothers, warn those who are idle, encourage the timid, help the weak, be patient with everyone. Make sure that nobody pays back wrong for wrong, but always try to be kind to each other and to everyone else. Be joyful always; pray continually; give thanks in all circumstances, for this is God's will for you in Christ Jesus" (1 Thessalonians 5:14-18).

In 2002 Rick Warren authored *The Purpose-Driven Life* which has sold more than twenty million copies in the first few years of publication—making it the best-selling hardback in U.S. history. The opening sentence of his book reads, "It's not about you." He continues to explain how our lives exist for God's purpose and the benefit of others, rather than our own gratification and self-absorption.

I find it both gratifying and compelling that a book written in the twenty-first century could open with such a statement and sell over twenty million copies! Perhaps this is because God's timeless truth for each of His unique creations is that true fulfillment can only be found by being others-focused—by consuming our lives with the discovery of our gifts and the deployment of those gifts for the benefit of others.

Pillar 3: Submissive

The Greek term used in James 3:17 for the submissive wisdom pillar is *eupeithes*, which means "easily obeying, compliant, submissive and obedient." It is a term that is very similar to *humility*, a word used by James in the prior two verses: "Who is wise and understanding among you? Let him show it by his good life, by deeds done in the humility that comes from wisdom" (James 3:13). James describes humility as having its true origin in wisdom. Submissiveness and humility go hand-in-hand and are treated as such in this chapter.

Humility and submissiveness are interdependent. Show me a person who claims to be humble but is not submissive, and I will show you a person who is not truly humble. Likewise, a person who acts submissively (rather than haughty by demanding his/her own way) is generally acting in humility. When the apostle Paul described love in 1 Corinthians 13:4-5, he mentioned that *love does not demand its own way"* (KJV). Christ, the embodiment of love, never displayed a lack of humility.

The wisdom pillar of submissiveness is completed in our lives when we are submissive to God and His principles of wisdom and we are truly humble in our interactions with others. Consider one of the key Proverbs verses on submissiveness:

Whoever corrects a mocker invites insult; whoever rebukes a wicked man incurs abuse. Do not rebuke a mocker or he will hate you; rebuke a wise man and he will love you. Instruct a wise man and he will be wiser still; teach a righteous man and he will add to his learning (Proverbs 9:7-9)

A companion verse is found in Psalm 141:5: "Let a righteous man strike me—it is a kindness; let him rebuke me—it is oil on my head. My head will not refuse it." The reason these verses are key to understanding the submissive wisdom pillar is because so many of us fall short in this area of submissiveness (that is, taking advice). Watching how people consider input from others is a fast way to discern how humble and submissive that person is. It's like taking an instant digital reading on their heart's level of humility. In fact I don't think I've ever met a truly humble and submissive person who didn't honor and appreciate input from others (no matter the source or how the message was delivered). On the flipside I've met plenty of people who showed their prideful hearts by not being open and willing to listen and consider input given by others.

Biblical submissiveness and humility are ultimately displayed by Christ's meekness—by His humility before God and His unwillingness to retaliate to man's injustices. Proverbs has much to say about this wisdom pillar.

Developing a Godly Response to Rebuke and Discipline

Proverbs:

- "Whoever corrects a mocker invites insult; whoever rebukes a wicked man incurs abuse. Do not rebuke a mocker or he will hate you; rebuke a wise man and he will love you. Instruct a wise man and he will be wiser still; teach a righteous man and he will add to his learning" (9:7-9).
- "He who listens to a life-giving rebuke will be at home among the wise" (15:31).
- "A rebuke impresses a man of discernment more than a hundred lashes a fool" (17:10).
- "When a mocker is punished, the simple gain wisdom; when a wise man is instructed, he gets knowledge" (21:11).
- "Like an earring of gold or an ornament of fine gold is a wise man's rebuke to a listening ear" (25:12).
- "A man who remains stiff-necked after many rebukes will suddenly be destroyed—without remedy" (29:1).

Developing a Godly Response to Rebuke

God occasionally sends us lessons, instructions or rebukes through people. Sometimes such instruction comes in nice, comfortable packages; other times, however, it comes in rough, harsh and candid packages. Should we pick and choose whom we listen to and accept advice from based upon how the message is packaged? That's not what these proverbs teach.

We all have the tendency to pick and choose the advice we accept based upon how the message is delivered. People are naturally defensive when they are rebuked. Is it because of pride? Fear of being hurt? Envy of the rebuker's position in life? Whatever the reason, oftentimes our first reaction to advice or correction is to "push back." We resist. "But what about you?" we snap. "Well— isn't this a good example of the pot calling the kettle black!" "Look who's talking!" And the list goes on. Our defensive response tends to be more certain when relating to family or to people we believe are somehow less experienced or qualified than we are.

But who are we *really* hurting by not listening to advice or correction? Often we're only hurting ourselves. Why do we put up a cold defense instead of accepting what someone has to say, especially if we know it is in our best interest to learn and grow from their input (regardless of how it was presented)?

When I was a youth, my mother offered me some coaching on how to handle friends who gave me harsh advice: "Son, just let their criticisms roll off your heart—just like water off a duck's back." My father offered similar advice for dealing with critics: "Even if only ten percent of what they say about you is true, just grow from that and ignore the rest." Colleagues I've worked with have advised me: "What doesn't kill you can only make you stronger—so just find a way to grow from their advice."

Perhaps there is some truth to all of these suggestions. When people offer us advice, caution or rebuke, it can make us stronger, live longer and live with more joy, peace and stability. But it depends on *how we take* the advice and whether we *choose* to grow from it or not.

How do you respond to people who offer you "gentle correction?" How about when they deliver a harsh rebuke? Constructive criticism? *Unconstructive* criticism? We need to train ourselves to *love others when rebuked, gain more wisdom when instructed* and *add to our learning when others teach us.* This is exactly what Proverbs 9:7-9 is teaching.

Developing a Godly Response to Discipline

Proverbs:

- **"He who heeds discipline shows the way to life, but whoever ignores correction leads others astray" (10:17).**
- **"Whoever loves discipline loves knowledge, but he who hates correction is stupid" (12:1).**
- **"He who ignores discipline comes to poverty and shame, but whoever heeds correction is honored" (13:18).**
- **"Stern discipline awaits him who leaves the path; he who hates correction will die" (15:10).**
- **"He who ignores discipline despises himself, but whoever heeds correction gains understanding" (15:32).**

I like to drive fast, especially when I'm by myself. The faster I can get some place, the better. The troubling thing about my habit is that it turns into willful sin when I'm watching my speedometer creep past the speed limit and knowingly keep it there.

Just a few weeks ago I was on a long three-hour drive returning from a business trip. Trying to get home in a hurry, I was pushing the speed limit. While I didn't get a ticket that day, the good Lord eventually allowed me to reap what I sowed! The next day I drove to work (a quick, three-mile drive) to pick up some paperwork. On my short drive back home I was ticketed for running a yellow light. The funny thing is that my guilt for this particular citation was actually questionable. The officer said he saw me enter the intersection after the light turned yellow by observing me through his rearview mirror, but I was already committed to the intersection when it turned yellow. None of this really mattered, though, as I did not have a clear conscience to argue with the officer. I knew I deserved a ticket, *if only because of my deeds the previous day.* I treated this circumstance like a "make-up call" that happens in sports.

I could mark this up to coincidence, but I chose not to. Rather I used this as an opportunity to change my behavior, and I am learning to enjoy more peaceful driving experiences.

Reflect

"And you have forgotten that word of encouragement that addresses you as sons: 'My son, do not make light of the Lord's discipline, and do not lose heart when he rebukes you, because the Lord disciplines those he loves, and he punishes everyone he accepts as a son.' Endure hardship as discipline; God is treating you as sons. For what son is not disciplined by his father?" (Hebrews 12:5-7).

Seeking Advice

Proverbs:

- "For lack of guidance a nation falls, but many advisers make victory sure" (11:14).
- "The plans of the righteous are just, but the advice of the wicked is deceitful" (12:5).
- "The way of a fool seems right to him, but a wise man listens to advice" (12:15).
- "Pride only breeds quarrels, but wisdom is found in those who take advice" (13:10).
- "Plans fail for lack of counsel, but with many advisers they succeed" (15:22).
- "Listen to advice and accept instruction, and in the end you will be wise" (19:20).
- "Make plans by seeking advice; if you wage war, obtain guidance" (20:18).
- "A wise man has great power, and a man of knowledge increases strength; for waging war you need guidance, and for victory many advisers" (24:5-6).

The book of Proverbs is about advice. Proverbs has thirty-one chapters and 915 verses with the goal of making a person wise. The very opening passage of the Bible's most widely read book (Psalms) advises God's people to *listen to the advice of the godly and avoid the counsel of the ungodly.*

The reason is that the very path of our lives is determined by the advice we choose to heed and act upon. At critical crossroads we can seek godly advice and by following it get on a course that leads to God's very best for us; or we can take advice from the world and open ourselves to certain destruction. The enemy loves to misdirect us, send us on "wild goose" chases and pull us away from God's best plans for our lives.

Proverbs 12:5 and Psalm 1:1-2 speak to this issue in very similar ways:

- "The plans of the righteous are just, but the advice of the wicked is deceitful" (Proverbs 12:5).
- "Blessed is the man who does not walk in the counsel of the wicked or stand in the way of sinners or sit in the seat of mockers. But his delight is in the law of the Lord, and on his law he meditates day and night" (Psalm 1:1-2).

How can we be sure to stay in God's plan and find His way for our lives? It's quite simple, actually. We accomplish this by some dos and don'ts. First, the don'ts. We don't *walk in the counsel of the wicked or stand in the way of sinners or sit in the seat of mockers.* Breaking this down, it means we don't:

- Walk *in* or order our lives *after* ungodly ways of living or ideals or seek after the values and aspirations of the world.
- Accept the deliberations and advice of the ungodly (Proverbs 1:10-19).
- Pattern our lives in habitual sin.
- Position ourselves in sinful ways, occupations, interests or hobbies.
- Mockingly and defiantly reject God's law (Proverbs 1:22).

The things we *do* are simple: We delight ourselves and meditate on God's Word. This is what the two passages above clearly teach. There is a reason why this practice works. Imagine having two identical dogs that are going to be entered in a dogfight in two weeks.

Which one will win the fight? The one you feed the most during the two weeks before the battle! It's the same thing with our minds. By filling ourselves with God's Word and by seeking and heeding godly counsel, we are preparing for spiritual victory. If we fill our minds and hearts with ungodly thoughts, values and pursuits, however, and follow the pattern and direction the world desires for our lives, we will experience spiritual defeat.

Our primary source of advice should be God's Word. The second source of advice is God's people. Regardless of rank, age, position or status, we need to listen to and consider advice from our peers and our subordinates as well as those over us. We all have "blinders" and often can't see where we need input, guidance and direction, and we need others—all kinds of others—to help us find and stay on God's course for our lives.

Even if we don't ultimately heed this advice, we need to be open to receiving it. In this way we value people by listening. We've all encountered leaders or friends who take the "my way or the highway" attitude when responding to input offered by others, but we still need to value and consider input from *all directions*. Some people bring creative input, while others bring critical input. In work settings I often see this with someone introducing a creative idea and others critiquing it. This is a necessary process that should be allowed to happen before making decisions about life choices, business decisions or career options. Allow the creative input to give birth to a new set of ideas or alternatives then let the critical input help you narrow the options so you can ultimately decide the best course of action.

How interesting it is that some people despise taking advice. In fact, giving advice is often seen as rude or even "politically incorrect." The Bible presents the opposite view, which is to *love* God's advice (the Word) and *actively seek out* the advice of the godly.

Submitting to
God's Hand of Providence

Proverbs:

- "Many are the plans in a man's heart, but it is the Lord's purpose that prevails" **(19:21).**
- "In his heart a man plans his course, but the Lord determines his steps" **(16:9).**

Biblical wisdom requires being submissive to God, the statutes and precepts of Scripture, and sometimes the advice of others. Sometimes being submissive to God requires that we humble ourselves and "roll with the punches" life throws us. In some circumstances such as temptation God wants us to fight, overcome and have victory. Other times God allows obstacles and burdens that far outweigh what we are able to bear. In these circumstances God wants us to succumb—to humble ourselves to the pressure so we are made more Christ-like—until He relieves the pressure.

The apostle Paul was a tenacious man, with amazing faith and resiliency. He cast out demons, broke down spiritual strongholds, destroyed arguments and had the resolute determination to march right back into a city and preach to those who had just stoned him and left him for dead outside the city gates. You couldn't find a more stubborn and persistent Christian in all of history. Yet he submitted, completely, to some type of physical ailment he just couldn't beat—*no matter how hard he tried or prayed*:

> To keep me from becoming conceited because of these surpassingly great revelations, there was given me a thorn in my flesh, a messenger of Satan, to torment me. Three times I pleaded with the Lord to take it away from me. But he said to me, "My grace is sufficient for you, for my power is made perfect in weakness." Therefore I will boast all the more gladly about my weaknesses, so that Christ's power may rest on me (2 Corinthians 12:7-9).

Many interpretations have been given about Paul's "thorn in the flesh" described in this passage, including impiety, temptation to unbelief, pains in the ear or head, epileptic fits or some other severe physical infirmity that was a hindrance to his ministry efforts (see 1 Corinthians 2:3; 2 Corinthians 10:10 and 11:30). Do you have, or have you had, a *thorn in your flesh* that just won't leave you alone? Perhaps this has come into your life to teach you a lesson that has eternal value. In the apostle Paul's case the thorn's purpose was to teach him to have total and complete dependence on Christ's power, that only in his complete weakness would Christ's power be at its fullest.

Sometimes thorns last for nearly a lifetime; other times they come for a season. I've had thorns that remained just long enough to deliver a lesson or "change in plans" that ultimately brought about God's best for my life. One such lesson came when our family decided to join other members of our church on a hike up Half Dome at Yosemite Valley in California. Half Dome is a granite mountaintop that rests 8,842 feet above sea level. Reaching the top requires ascending 4,700 feet during a grueling seventeen-mile round-trip hike that takes twelve to fourteen hours of sheer leg power and will. Knowing that such a feat would mandate preparation, my ten-year-old daughter and I began getting in shape about two months before the hike. We went on long bike rides, enjoyed shorter hikes, ate healthy food and geared up in every way possible.

The week before the hike I had a business trip to the East Coast that required long days and flights that threw me for a loop. I developed an ear infection that left me feeling half-dead at the Chicago airport, where I had to wait long hours for delayed flights to take me home. When I finally arrived home I was very sick and in no condition for the hike. I tried praying. I tried resting. Nothing seemed to work. When the day of the hike arrived and the hikers left at 5:00 a.m. to start up the mountain, I found myself in no condition for the adventure, so I remained at the campsite nursing my ringing ears and head cold. I submitted to my "thorn" for that trip. But rather than questioning why God allowed this gray cloud to cover me I made the best of it, submitted to the situation and sought out what He would have me do for the day.

As things turned out I spent the time on my laptop authoring an article that ended up being a major success for my career. I knew God wanted me to write the article, but my busy life had not yet allowed me the opportunity to get it done. So He parked me at a campsite with nothing to do for twelve hours but write the article. God is good. Maybe I will get to hike the mountain another time, but for that trip God had planned a different mountain for me to climb.

Sometimes the impact of "thorns" is worse than just missing a day hike. We might make plans. We might have dreams. But the wisdom principle outlined in Proverbs transcends all situations. The Lord will have His way. While seeking a certain goal we have in mind, we might fall short of "hitting *our* mark" but end up hitting the precise mark God wanted us to hit all along.

Proverbs 16:9 tells us, "In his heart a man plans his course, but the Lord determines his steps." So, while we might have "many plans in our hearts," the Lord's purpose will ultimately prevail. When we think life has gone awry, rest assured knowing that "in all things God works for the good of those who love him, who have been called according to his purpose" (Romans 8:28).

Assume a Position of Humility Before You Are Assigned One

Proverbs:

- "When pride comes, then comes disgrace, but with humility comes wisdom" (11:2).
- "The fear of the Lord teaches a man wisdom, and humility comes before honor" (15:33).
- "Pride goes before destruction, a haughty spirit before a fall" (16:18).
- "Before his downfall a man's heart is proud, but humility comes before honor" (18:12).

I've been on two rafting trips I will never forget. These trips were separated by twenty years, and they occurred during completely different eras of my life. I went on the first trip when I was young and bold, and the second trip occurred when I had gained a little more maturity.

On the first trip I was nineteen years old and full of myself. I persuaded two of my friends to join me on a "Huck Finn" adventure down the American River by convincing them we could build a raft made of logs strapped together with rope then float downriver about ten miles to our final destination. The first step of our expedition was to swim across the river about a hundred yards upriver from a place known as the San Juan Rapids. This is the part of the American

River that rafters enjoy the most—two hundred yards of white water rapids.

Thinking we could swim across before being swept down into the rapids, we plunged into the cold water. We were all somewhat experienced swimmers and reasonably fit (at least, so we thought); but it took only ten seconds of fighting the current before we were forced into plan B, which was holding our breath and praying for our very lives. We couldn't touch bottom, and the current was much stronger than we expected. It began pulling us straight for the rapids, which was no place to be without a life jacket.

I watched my friends, Dan and Andy, disappear under a mass of frothy water downriver. I kept fighting to reach the other side, and finally my feet found the bottom, just ten yards short of being pulled into the rapids myself. Upon reaching the shore my surroundings turned orange, and tunnel vision began to set in as my body went into shock. All I could think about was Dan and Andy, who were nowhere in sight. I was too numb—emotionally and physically—to yell for them. Two minutes earlier I had been a happy-go-lucky, prideful young man ready to conquer the world, but now I was just a washed-up ball of flesh who thought he had led his good friends to their demise.

All I could do was stare downriver in hopes of seeing them, but no sign came for what seemed like ten minutes. Then, walking up the other side of the river, came Dan and Andy. They were able to survive their two-hundred-yard trek down the rapids by gulping air in between sets of rapids. Shaken to the core, we hiked to the nearest road and began searching for a payphone to summon a ride home. Remarkably we ran into my girlfriend (and soon-to-be wife) driving home from her day at college (yes, she's always been the more responsible one!). She gave us a ride home, and I sat sheepishly in her car knowing I had no business taking such useless risks in life if I hoped to settle down and be a dependable husband someday.

That day our pride and self-assuredness were washed away by the very river that had almost stolen our lives. Nothing kept us alive but the grace of God. We were just plain blessed to have our lives spared. We had all experienced the promise offered by Proverbs— pride comes before a fall.

The second rafting trip occurred almost twenty years later and was markedly different from the first one. The river we journeyed was filled with Class III+ rapids—some of which came in quick succession with little recovery time. Despite being much more treacherous than the rapids I had experienced twenty years earlier, this trip was actually safe *and* enjoyable because of three distinct differences. First, we had a professional guide who knew the river very well; second, we had the proper gear, which included a solid commercial raft and fitted life vests; and, third, we relied on team-work to maneuver through the obstacles. By listening carefully to the orders issued by the guide ("two forward," "three back," "forward easy," and so on), we worked in unison to navigate the dangerous river. Lacking any one of these three factors, the trip could have easily turned into an experience like the first trip, or worse.

By having a humble spirit and acknowledging our need for a guide, using proper gear and relying on the help of others, we were able to journey through even more treacherous rapids *and* enjoy them. Class III rapids are defined as "large, continuous series or sets of waves, complete with 'holes' and 'undercurrents,' small drops, ledges and waterfalls." Isn't life just like Class III rapids some-times? To survive the "rapids of life," we need to humble ourselves by submitting to *The Guide*, properly prepare for the occasion, apply teamwork and rely on others.

Submitting to God's Plan and Patiently Waiting for Wisdom's Blessing

Proverbs:

- "The sluggard craves and gets nothing, but the desires of the diligent are fully satisfied" (13:4).
- "A sluggard does not plow in season; so at harvest time he looks but finds nothing" (20:4).
- "The sluggard's craving will be the death of him, because his hands refuse to work. All day long he craves for more, but the righteous give without sparing" (21:25-26).

Living a life ruled by godly wisdom doesn't always seem to pay off right away. In fact, to experience the true benefits of living a life governed by godly wisdom, you need to live by its principles for a long time. True, godly wisdom is not just concerned about the "now"—it's concerned with the *long run*.

This is because life is about the principle of *sowing* and *reaping* (what a farmer does when planting and harvesting crops). We are all farmers, whether we choose to be or not, and we all have two fields: one for the good seeds we plant; the other for the bad. The wise choices and actions we make are deposited in the good field, and all the rest in the "other field."

God's principles of sowing, waiting and reaping are found throughout the Scriptures. God desires that we faithfully submit to Him and wait on Him for the results of our actions to spring up into positive results. As sure as the sun comes up, as sure as we breathe, as sure as what goes up must come down, so sowing and reaping are a fact of life.

- We can sow good or sow evil, and it comes back: "Do not be deceived: God cannot be mocked. A man reaps what he sows. The one who sows to please his sinful nature, from that nature will reap destruction; the one who sows to please the Spirit, from the Spirit will reap eternal life" (Galatians 6:7-8).
- We sow words of faith or words of unbelief, and those very words can influence our future: "If any of you lacks wisdom, he should ask God, who gives generously to all without finding fault, and it will be given to him. But when he asks, he must believe and not doubt, because he who doubts is like a wave of the sea, blown and tossed by the wind" (James 1:5-6). "And without faith it is *impossible* to please God, because anyone who comes to him must believe that he exists and that he rewards those who earnestly seek him" (Hebrews 11:6).
- If we sow evil, evil comes back. If we live for Christ, blessings come back. "If a man pays back evil for good, evil will never leave his house" (Proverbs 17:13). "Let us not become weary in doing good, for at the proper time we will reap a harvest if we do not give up" (Galatians 6:9).
- We can sow to the flesh and destroy our lives, or we can sow to the Spirit and receive God's blessings: "For the sinful nature desires what is contrary to the Spirit, and the Spirit what is contrary to the sinful nature. They are in conflict with each other, so that you do not do what you want. . . . The acts of the sinful nature are obvious: sexual immorality, impurity and debauchery; idolatry and witchcraft; hatred, discord, jealousy, fits of rage, selfish ambition, dissensions, factions and envy; drunkenness, orgies,

and the like. . . . But the fruit of the Spirit is love, joy, peace, patience, kindness, goodness, faithfulness, gentleness, and self-control. Against such things there is no law" (Galatians 5:17-23).

- We can sow our finances to God, and He will bless us. We can cheat God and lose out on His blessings for our lives: "Honor the Lord with your wealth, with the firstfruits of all your crops; then your barns will be filled to overflowing, and your vats will brim over with new wine" (Proverbs 3:9-10). "'Bring the whole tithe into the storehouse, that there may be food in my house. Test me in this,' says the Lord Almighty, 'and see if I will not throw open the floodgates of heaven and pour out so much blessing that you will not have room enough for it'" (Malachi 3:10).
- Sow your life to Christ, give Him control of your life, and you will have blessings eternal and blessings in this life: "'I tell you the truth,' Jesus replied, 'no one who has left home or brothers or sisters or mother or father or children or fields for me and the gospel will fail to receive a hundred times as much in this present age (homes, brothers, sisters, mothers, children and fields—and with them, persecutions) and in the age to come, eternal life'" (Mark 10:29-30).

All of these promises and blessings require our investment, time and sacrifice. We need to submit to God and trust that living by His promises and wisdom's principles will pay off in lasting and meaningful ways in our lives. Remember...only God sees and knows the big picture.

Pillar 4: Merciful

The Greek term used in James 3:17 for the merciful wisdom pillar is *eleos*, which means "having kindness or good will toward the miserable and the afflicted; practicing the virtue of mercy; showing one's self merciful toward men; or the moral quality of feeling compassion and showing kindness toward someone in need." Consider how Christ defined mercy in the parable of the unmerciful servant (Matthew 18:21-35):

> Then Peter came to Jesus and asked, "Lord, how many times shall I forgive my brother when he sins against me? Up to seven times?" Jesus answered, "I tell you, not seven times, but seventy-seven times. Therefore, the kingdom of heaven is like a king who wanted to settle accounts with his servants. As he began the settlement, a man who owed him ten thousand talents was brought to him. Since he was not able to pay, the master ordered that he and his wife and his children and all that he had be sold to repay the debt. The servant fell on his knees before him. 'Be patient with me,' he begged, 'and I will pay back everything.' The servant's master took pity on him, canceled the debt and let him go. But when that servant went out, he found one of his fellow servants who owed him a hundred denari. He grabbed him and began to choke him. 'Pay back what you owe me!' he demanded. His fellow servant fell to his knees and begged him, 'Be patient with me, and I will pay you back.' But he

refused. Instead, he went off and had the man thrown into prison until he could pay the debt. When the other servants saw what had happened, they were greatly distressed and went and told their master everything that had happened. Then the master called the servant in. 'You wicked servant,' he said, 'I canceled all that debt of yours because you begged me to. Shouldn't you have had mercy on your fellow servant just as I had on you?' In anger his master turned him over to the jailers to be tortured, until he should pay back all he owed. This is how my heavenly Father will treat each of you unless you forgive your brother from your heart."

Who are we to withhold mercy from others if our Lord Jesus extended His whole life for us on the cross? The parable above gives us all the reasons we need to choose mercy.

Like the other six pillars of wisdom in James 3:17, mercy is established along a continuum with justice on the other side. For this reason, verses from Proverbs that deal with both mercy and justice are discussed in this chapter.

Loving the Poor

Proverbs:

- "He who is kind to the poor lends to the Lord, and he will reward him for what he has done" (19:17).
- "If a man shuts his ears to the cry of the poor, he too will cry out and not be answered" (21:13).

God cares deeply about the poor. There are hundreds of verses in the Bible about the poor and God's heart for them. The two verses above show how God's promises are *specific* to our lives and are intertwined with our *choices*—including *how we respond to the poor* He places in our life circle. Consider Christ's expressions of love for the poor:

> Looking at his disciples, he said: "Blessed are you who are poor, for yours is the kingdom of God. Blessed are you who hunger now, for you will be satisfied. Blessed are you who weep now, for you will laugh" (Luke 6:20-21).

> Then the righteous will answer him, "Lord, when did we see you hungry and feed you, or thirsty and give you something to drink? When did we see you a stranger and invite you in, or needing clothes and clothe you? When did we see you sick or in prison and go to visit you?" The King will reply, "I tell

you the truth, whatever you did for one of the least of these brothers of mine, you did for me" (Matthew 25:37-40).

By loving the poor, we love God—it's that simple. Mother Teresa once said, "Only in heaven will we see how much we owe to the poor for helping us to love God better because of them."

The longer you live a Christian life, the more you will see that God brings you the "poor" in many *different forms*. They come to us poor in spirit, in heart, in health, in hope, as well as financially poor. In fact, some of the richest people you know might be *poor in spirit*. There are also several ways we can love the poor. When giving our money, time, listening ear, touch or encouraging words, we must be sensitive to the Holy Spirit's prompting so we can wisely know *whom* to give to and *how* to give.

We also need to learn perhaps the most difficult lesson about giving—knowing *if* we should give. Sometimes giving money to those in need can *hinder* more than it can *help* because giving money to people who refuse to change their irresponsible spending habits can be a huge mistake (now they'll just be spending your money unwisely!). Working with your church's benevolence group and consulting other resources can help you answer the "if" question about giving. Some biblically sound benevolence guidelines are published by Crown Financial Ministries and can be found online at www.crown.org.

When it comes to giving (especially financial giving), many are quick to put up defenses: "The poor are poor because of their own bad choices. . . . Why don't they just pull themselves together, start working for a living, go from one good job to a better job and build a successful life like I did? If this is how I did it in life, why should it be any different for them?"

First, this line of thinking is stereotypical. While these assumptions may be true about some, they are not necessarily true about many of the people who are currently in need. Second, you really have *no idea* how they arrived at their place in life. Whether or not we would like to admit this, there is a chance we would have been even worse off if we had lived their lives! Third, let's imagine these assumptions are completely true about the particular poor that God has placed in your life. Does this mean we shouldn't have mercy and grace on them? We must be mindful of the proverb: "If a man shuts his ears to the cry of the poor, he too will cry out and not be answered" (21:13).

We can apply these truths to our lives by considering every encounter with others as divine appointments: "For we are God's workmanship, created in Christ Jesus to do good works, which God prepared *in advance* for us to do" (Ephesians 2:10). Where will your feet take you? How will you respond the next time God brings you the poor, in whatever form they come? When the Lord scribed Proverbs 19:17 through Solomon ("He who is kind to the poor lends to the Lord, and he will reward him for what he has done"), He was making a very straightforward proposal: "*You* help the poor, and *I* will repay you."

Reflect

Let us touch the dying, the poor, the lonely and the unwanted according to the graces we have received and **let us not be ashamed or slow** to do the humble work. —Mother Teresa

"Religion that God our Father accepts as pure and faultless is this: to look after orphans and widows in their distress and to keep oneself from being polluted by the world" (James 1:27).

Active Mercy

Proverbs:

- "He who is kind to the poor lends to the Lord, and he will reward him for what he has done" (19:17).
- "If a man shuts his ears to the cry of the poor, he too will cry out and not be answered" (21:13).
- "The righteous care about justice for the poor, but the wicked have no such concern" (29:7).
- "Speak up for those who cannot speak for themselves, for the rights of all who are destitute. Speak up and judge fairly; defend the rights of the poor and needy" (31:8-9).

We tend to think of mercy as having sympathy toward someone or forgiving someone who has wronged us. But sometimes it means spending our strength for the benefit of others. That is, mercy should be actively and deliberately deployed; it is not just a response of "looking the other way" when wronged.

In fact, the Greek term used for mercy, *eleos*, in James 3:17 means so much more than mercy as we tend to understand it. Its meaning includes *having kindness or good will toward the miserable and the afflicted* and *the moral quality of feeling compassion and especially of showing kindness toward someone in need.*

In fact, the Bible gives some wonderful examples of this concept of "mercy in action." One such example is found in Isaiah 58 when the Lord describes the type of fasting He prefers. Typically, people think of fasting as going without food for a period of prayer or meditation. This is certainly one type of fasting. But in the Isaiah passage the Lord describes another type of fasting as *an active pursuit of justice and help for those in need.*

Before describing this type of fasting, He first contrasts it with the kind of fasting He *despises.*

> "Why have we fasted," they say, "and you have not seen it? Why have we humbled ourselves, and you have not noticed?" Your fasting ends in quarreling and strife and in striking each other with wicked fists. You cannot fast as you do today and expect your voice to be heard on high. Is this the kind of fast I have chosen, only a day for a man to humble himself? Is it only for bowing one's head like a reed and for lying on sackcloth and ashes? Is that what you call a fast, a day acceptable to the Lord? (Isaiah 58:3-5).

Now compare this with the kind of active and merciful fasting the Lord *prefers.*

> Is not this the kind of fasting I have chosen: to loose the chains of injustice and untie the cords of the yoke, to set the oppressed free and break every yoke? Is it not to share your food with the hungry and to provide the poor wanderer with shelter—when you see the naked, to clothe him, and not to turn away from your own flesh and blood? Then your light will break forth like the dawn, and your healing will quickly appear; then your righteousness will go before you, and the glory of the Lord will be your rear guard. Then you will call, and the Lord will answer; you will cry for help, and he will say: Here am I. If you do away with the yoke of oppression, with the pointing finger and malicious talk, and if you spend yourselves in behalf of the hungry and satisfy the needs of the oppressed, then your light will rise in the darkness, and your night will become like the noonday. The Lord will guide you always; he will satisfy your needs in a

sun-scorched land and will strengthen your frame. You will be like a well-watered garden, like a spring whose waters never fail (Isaiah 58:6-11).

The passage above shows that we should *actively* use our strength and resources while we're here on this planet! Would the Lord have it any other way than for us to take our strengths, talents, resources and time for investing in others who are in need? Isn't that one primary reason why the good Lord allows breath in our lungs today?

Consider again these proverbs and others. They are direct promises from the *God of heaven* to those who will take these commands seriously.

- "He who is kind to the poor lends to the Lord, and he will reward him for what he has done" (Proverbs 19:17).
- "Blessed are the merciful, for they will be shown mercy" (Matthew 5:7).
- "If a man shuts his ears to the cry of the poor, he too will cry out and not be answered" (Proverbs 21:13).
- "Speak up for those who cannot speak for themselves, for the rights of all who are destitute. Speak up and judge fairly; defend the rights of the poor and needy" (31:8-9).
- "And if you spend yourselves in behalf of the hungry and satisfy the needs of the oppressed, then your light will rise in the darkness, and your night will become like the noonday. The Lord will guide you always; he will satisfy your needs in a sun-scorched land and will strengthen your frame. You will be like a well-watered garden, like a spring whose waters never fail" (Isaiah 58:10-11).

Do you *really* believe God when it comes to these verses? That God will repay you for lending to the poor? That your own cry will not be heard if you shut your ears to the poor? That you should defend the rights of the poor and needy? Truly, these are the *ways* of wisdom.

Acts of Kindness

Proverbs:

- "A kindhearted woman gains respect, but ruthless men gain only wealth. A kind man benefits himself, but a cruel man brings trouble on himself" (11:16-17).
- "An anxious heart weighs a man down, but a kind word cheers him up" (12:25).
- "He who despises his neighbor sins, but blessed is he who is kind to the needy. Do not those who plot evil go astray? But those who plan what is good find love and faithfulness" (14:21-22).
- "He who oppresses the poor shows contempt for their Maker, but whoever is kind to the needy honors God" (14:31).

I'd like to illustrate biblical kindness using two stories about taxi cab drivers. The first is a story shared by Charles Swindoll (2006) that demonstrates the importance of kindness, which I have summarized below.

While on a taxi run as a young man, Charles drove to pick up a passenger at 2:30 a.m. Upon arriving at the house, he was greeted by an elderly woman in her 80s, wearing a pillbox hat and dressed as if she were right out of a 1940s movie. He glanced inside her house and noticed furniture covered with sheets, no clocks or utensils, and a small box containing some personal belongings. Taking only her vintage nylon suitcase to the car, he began the journey to her destination.

She requested that he drive through the center of town on the way to her final destination (a hospice) so she could reminisce while driving through "memory lane" in her old neighborhood. She explained that she didn't have any family left and the doctor told her she had only a short time left to live. Upon hearing this, Charles turned off the taxi meter and spent two hours driving her through the neighborhood where she lived as a child. She pointed out the places she had worked as a young adult, old warehouses that used to be dance halls and all her favorite pastimes.

As the sun began to come up, she grew tired and asked to be taken to the hospice. When they arrived, two helpers hurried her into a wheelchair as Charles carried her suitcase to the door. When she asked Charles how much she owed him for the drive, he replied, "Nothing," and embraced her with a warm hug. She held on tightly and thanked him for giving an old woman a little moment of joy in the last days of her life. He squeezed her hand good-bye and walked into the dim morning light. As the doors shut behind him, he realized it was the closing of her life.

He picked up no more passengers the rest of that shift but instead drove aimlessly, lost in thought. Reflecting on this occasion in his life, he believes it is one of the most important things he's ever done. He pondered, "What if that woman had gotten an angry driver? One who was anxious to end his shift? One who was cold or rude?" He concludes this story by admonishing: "Is it any wonder after hearing that story that one of the qualities that God expects of those who claim the name of Christ is that we be people of love and kindness?"

The second "taxi story" is about a ride I recently had while traveling on the East Coast. After finishing a speaking engagement, I asked the receptionist to call for a taxi cab to drive me to my hotel. Not having the exact street address of my hotel but knowing it was an airport hotel, I gave her the name of the hotel airport, assuming the hotel would be just a couple of miles from the airport.

When the cab arrived and the driver learned I wasn't actually going to the airport but to a hotel that was near the airport, he became quite upset because this would take him off of his regular airport route, causing him lost time and money. He grudgingly took me to the hotel and, toward the end of the drive, wouldn't even speak with me. Despite the fact that his customer service was terrible, I tipped him well and apologized for the misunderstanding. Upon hearing my apology and glaring at the generous tip I placed in his hand, he stood in front of me, shocked, for a few seconds. He bowed in humility, handed me my bag and wished me a good day. I have no doubt he spent the rest of the day reflecting on my gesture of kindness.

I didn't have to respond this way. I could have refused to tip him and probably been justified. But what would have been accomplished by doing this? The result of this would have been sending two angry people (him and me) into the world that day. But for an extra ten dollars with some humility the situation was redeemed, and two appreciative men went on with their lives.

Acts of kindness often take so little time. But they can have such huge returns. Proverbs 18:16 shares, "A gift opens the way for the giver and ushers him into the presence of the great." What gifts of your time and resources do you have to share? Sometimes giving gifts of time and resources—if done sincerely—can open ways that appear closed.

What opportunities to provide acts of kindness have you overlooked lately? Conducting acts of kindness is easier for some than others. Some people are just plain wired to look out for others. Others need to work hard at developing a "radar" system that scans for the needs of others and acts accordingly.

Mixing Mercy and Money:
Knowing When *Not* to
Give Money to Those in Need

Proverbs:

- "Go to the ant, you sluggard; consider its ways and be wise! It has no commander, no overseer or ruler, yet it stores its provisions in summer and gathers its food at harvest. How long will you lie there, you sluggard? When will you get up from your sleep? A little sleep, a little slumber, a little folding of the hands to rest—and poverty will come on you like a bandit and scarcity like an armed man" (6:6-11).
- "The way of the sluggard is blocked with thorns, but the path of the upright is a highway" (15:19).
- "The sluggard buries his hand in the dish; he will not even bring it back to his mouth!" (19:24).
- "A sluggard does not plow in season; so at harvest time he looks but finds nothing" (20:4).
- "The sluggard says, 'There is a lion outside!' or, 'I will be murdered in the streets!'" (22:13).
- "I went past the field of the sluggard, past the vineyard of the man who lacks judgment; thorns had come up everywhere, the ground was covered with weeds, and the stone wall was in ruins. I applied my heart to what I observed and learned a lesson from what I saw: A

little sleep, a little slumber, a little folding of the hands to rest—and poverty will come on you like a bandit and scarcity like an armed man" (24:30-34).

- **"The sluggard says, 'There is a lion in the road, a fierce lion roaming the streets!' As a door turns on its hinges, so a sluggard turns on his bed. The sluggard buries his hand in the dish; he is too lazy to bring it back to his mouth. The sluggard is wiser in his own eyes than seven men who answer discreetly" (26:13-16).**

How should we extend love and mercy to those who *will not* work but claim they need our financial support? To those who have the *ability* and *opportunity* to work (for God has said that mankind will earn their living by the *sweat* of their brow; see Genesis 3:17-19) but have come into financial difficulties because they have *not done their part to earn a living*?

Consider a friend or relative who has amassed credit card debt and can hardly keep up with monthly payments. If you won the lottery tomorrow, should you pay their credit cards as a gift? Sure—go right ahead—just be prepared to do it again in six months! Canceling their credit card debt will not necessarily cancel the behaviors that caused the debt in the first place. Don't get me wrong—if the Lord clearly leads you to make such an act, do it. Just be sure it's really God leading you.

Another drawback that would likely come from canceling your friend's credit card debt is that, unless they are able and willing to change their spending behaviors, you can stunt their growth and maturity in the area of financial management. What good will come from having liposuction performed to drop twenty pounds of excess weight in a single day if the eating habits that created the weight problem are not also changed?

The Bible takes idle living very seriously. God is not pleased with those who squander their God-given talents, abilities and opportunities by being a "sluggard" as referenced in the proverbs above. Sometimes even resting and recuperating in front of the TV after work can constitute slothfulness. For example, Ecclesiastes 11:6

encourages us to make the most of *all* our time, even every moment: "Sow your seed in the morning, and at evening let not your hands be idle, for you do not know which will succeed, whether this or that, or whether both will do equally well." If you have talents—and God knows that you do—put them into service, and you will do well in life. The apostle Paul chimes into this discussion with a similar admonition.

Reflect

"In the name of the Lord Jesus Christ, we command you, brothers, to keep away from every brother who is idle and does not live according to the teaching you received from us. For you yourselves know how you ought to follow our example. We were not idle when we were with you, nor did we eat anyone's food without paying for it. On the contrary, we worked night and day, laboring and toiling so that we would not be a burden to any of you. We did this, not because we do not have the right to such help, but in order to make ourselves a model for you to follow. For even when we were with you, we gave you this rule: 'If a man will not work, he shall not eat.' We hear that some among you are idle. They are not busy; they are busybodies. Such people we command and urge in the Lord Jesus Christ to settle down and earn the bread they eat. And as for you, brothers, never tire of doing what is right. If anyone does not obey our instruction in this letter, take special note of him. Do not associate with him, in order that he may feel ashamed. Yet do not regard him as an enemy, but warn him as a brother" (2 Thessalonians 3:6-15).

"Make it your ambition to lead a quiet life, to mind your own business and to work with your hands, just as we told you, so that your daily life may win the respect of outsiders and so that you will not be dependent on anybody" (1 Thessalonians 4:11-12).

Looking the Other Way

Proverbs:

- "Hatred stirs up dissension, but love covers over all wrongs" (10:12).
- "He who covers over an offense promotes love, but whoever repeats the matter separates close friends" (17:9).
- "Do not gloat when your enemy falls; when he stumbles, do not let your heart rejoice, or the Lord will see and disapprove and turn his wrath away from him" (24:17-18).
- "If your enemy is hungry, give him food to eat; if he is thirsty, give him water to drink. In doing this, you will heap burning coals on his head, and the Lord will reward you" (25:21-22).

We all have opportunities to overlook wrongdoings made against us. Ranging from small infractions to major violations—we all have bad things happen to us through the actions of others. The four verses above can be broken down into two sets of "proverbial pairs" (sets of proverbs on the same topic) that speak about being merciful to others in various ways. Each of these sets will be discussed in turn below.

Covering an Offense with Love

Verses 10:12 and 17:9 relate to covering an offense with love. This is one of the classic expressions of mercy—responding in love when we could have responded with anger or looking the other way when we could have sought vengeance. We are also encouraged by Peter the disciple in this way: "Above all, love each other deeply, because *love covers over a multitude of sins*" (1 Peter 5:8). This was demonstrated by Christ in the most selfless way when, while hanging on a cross, He said to His persecutors, "Father, forgive them, for they know not what they do" (Luke 23:34).

Looking the other way when someone breaks the law or acts unethically is, of course, *not* what these verses are teaching. When the Lord allows us to witness or personally experience others whom we *know* are breaking the law, we are expected to act. I just experienced this personally when one of our clients had to terminate two employees: one for changing employment test scores for a few "select" candidates; the other who knew about it but said nothing. Both were in the wrong. God expects us to live uprightly—no matter what the cost. Sins that break laws based on things we do or things we overlook or ignore are still sin to the One to whom we must give an account. Matthew 10:26 encourages us in this regard: "There is nothing concealed that will not be disclosed, or hidden that will not be made known."

Relating to Your Enemies

Verses 24:17-18 and 25:21-22 are proverbial pairs that deal with relating to your enemies. Verse 25:22 describes "heaping burning coals" on your enemy's head by feeding him and offering him drink. This verse offers an interesting set of promises to us when we put into action what it suggests.

First, the enemy will be punished by this action (that is, with burning coals heaped on his head, a punishment that is reserved for the wicked—see Psalm 140:10). Second, our enemy will perhaps be won over by our loving action, which is our ultimate goal. By extending kindness to your enemy, you may cause him to repent or change. Christ speaks to this point directly in the Sermon on the Mount (Matthew 5:43-48):

> You have heard that it was said, "Love your neighbor and hate your enemy." But I tell you: Love your enemies and pray for those who persecute you, that you may be sons of your Father in heaven. He causes his sun to rise on the evil and the good, and sends rain on the righteous and the unrighteous. If you love those who love you, what reward will you get? Are not even the tax collectors doing that? And if you greet only your brothers, what are you doing more than others? Do not even pagans do that? Be perfect, therefore, as your heavenly Father is perfect.

Third, notice that this second set of proverbs (25:22) states that *the Lord will reward you* for the kindness you extend to the enemy. This is one really good reason for overlooking the wrongdoings others commit against us. We should focus on living for God and pleasing Him as our *only audience.* We should not fear our enemies or any other mortal person more than God. This is difficult especially when we cannot see God but can see people. But Christ encourages us: "Do not be afraid of those who kill the body but cannot kill the soul. Rather, be afraid of the one who can destroy both soul and body in hell" (Matthew 10:28). We should fear God, not man: "Fear of man will prove to be a snare, but whoever trusts in the Lord is kept safe" (Proverbs 29:25). May the Lord encourage us to live with this long-term perspective—for the game does not end when we are finished on earth but continues much, much beyond.

Pillar 5: Fruitful

The Greek term used to describe the fruitful (or "good fruit") wisdom pillar in James 3:17 is *karpon agathon*, which means: "Fruit of the trees, vines, of the fields, the fruit of one's loins (children); or an effect, result, work, act, deed, advantage, profit or a 'reaped' harvest." When it comes to living a Christ-like life, "good fruit" includes both *receiving* and *bearing* good fruit. Having a fruitful life means the same thing today as it did two thousand years ago when the New Testament was written: Good fruit is *sweet* (enjoyable to all) and *comes in a wide variety*. The interesting thing about fruit is that it is not manufactured or cooked in the microwave—it has to be *grown*. Good fruit is grown and cultivated through hard work, diligence and perseverance.

Good fruit will not produce a righteous life, for there are plenty of worldly people who are bearing "good fruit." A righteous life, however, results in bearing good fruit. Good fruit is a necessity for wisdom and is therefore a pillar, because wisdom both *exists for* and is *proven by* good works.

Money—as a fruit of our hard work and discipline—is not the only good fruit of our lives, but it is the most versatile because so much can be done with it. For this reason and because Proverbs includes a great deal of discussion about financial fruitfulness, this chapter is limited to this same topic.

Tithing

Proverbs:

- **"Honor the Lord with your wealth, with the *firstfruits* of all your crops; then your barns will be filled to overflowing, and your vats will brim over with new wine" (3:9-10).**

Tithing is an *action* word that means *giving one-tenth*. By giving ten percent of our income—right off the top—we put God first in the financial area of our lives. God blesses us financially when we put Him first by tithing! When considering whether to tithe ten percent based on your gross or net income (before or after taxes), just choose which of these you would rather God bless you by.

I'm not talking about prosperity theology, which teaches that we can be made *rich* by tithing and that God is some type of great money machine in the sky who will rain down abundant funds. I am speaking about the promise God makes in the passage above to bless us with *abundant provision* (not to be confused with flashy wealth or riches) when we put Him first in our finances. God blesses us with provisions above our basic needs *so we can share it*.

We need to be careful about this distinction. God has no desire to grant us abundance to be completely consumed by our personal desires. James warns about this: "When you ask, you do not receive, because you ask with wrong motives, that you may spend what you get on your pleasures" (James 4:3). Proverbs 30:7-9 also speaks to this: "Two things I ask of you, O Lord? Do not refuse me before I die: Keep falsehood and lies far from me; give me neither poverty nor riches, but give me only my daily bread. Otherwise, I may have too much and disown you and say, 'Who is the Lord?' Or I may become poor and steal, and so dishonor the name of my God."

When we have this distinction straight and honor God continually by placing Him first in the area of our finances, He is free to bless us abundantly. One need not look any further than the verse above to know this. But just to be sure, Malachi 3:10-11 and 2 Corinthians 9:6-7 share the same voice in this promise.

- "Bring the whole tithe into the storehouse, that there may be food in my house. 'Test me in this,' says the Lord Almighty, 'and see if I will not throw open the floodgates of heaven and pour out so much blessing that you will not have room enough for it. I will prevent pests from devouring your crops, and the vines in your fields will not cast their fruit,' says the Lord Almighty" (Malachi 3:10-11).
- "Remember this: Whoever sows sparingly will also reap sparingly, and whoever sows generously will also reap generously. Each man should give what he has decided in his heart to give, not reluctantly or under compulsion, for God loves a cheerful giver. And God is able to make all grace abound to you, so that in all things at all times, having all that you need, you will abound in every good work" (2 Corinthians 9:6-8).

In these passages there are two important promises. First, there is God's commitment of abundant provision to those who put Him first in their finances. Second, God will protect what we have—all He has given—from the devourer: "I will prevent pests from devouring your crops, and the vines in your fields will not cast their fruit" (Malachi 3:11).

There is a reason God wants us to give the *firstfruits*—the very first "cut" from the top of our income. God wants and deserves the very best. He doesn't deserve the leftovers. There are other reasons as well.

- Tithing teaches us, on a regular basis, that we are to put God first in our finances. In this way tithing is a spiritual act of worship.
- Because tithing is a flat rate (that is, ten percent) and a consistent part of our giving, it teaches us to realize God will be first priority in all of our increase or decrease in earnings. By consistently and regularly giving ten percent (or more), we are realizing it all belongs to Him—no matter how much or how little we make.
- Tithing keeps the grip of materialism away from our hearts by narrowing our income and automatically directing some of our funds to the church.
- By tithing now, we pass blessings into our future (Matthew 6:19-21).
- We cannot out-give God. Being faithful to God allows Him to show His faithfulness toward us.
- God desires to give perfect gifts to His children (James 1:17). Giving opens the way for God to bless us in very special ways.
- The more we practice giving to others, the more we receive from him. It really is better to give than to receive (Luke 6:38).

There really is something *miraculous* about tithing. Without exaggeration I have experienced dozens of miracles in my life by putting God first in my finances. But don't take my word or anyone else's on the matter—tithing is a very personal thing between you and God, and it's the only issue in Scripture where God asks us to *test Him* (Malachi 3:10). Let God prove Himself real and faithful to you by trusting Him and obeying in this area.

By placing God first in your finances through tithing, we mobilize spiritual powers and principles that transcend the limits and boundaries of this physical world. Putting God first in our finances allows God's fullest blessing in our lives. If you don't believe me, ask someone who's been tithing faithfully for several years. Their stories will amaze you, I promise.

Reflect

"The Lord will send a blessing on your barns and on everything you put your hand to. The Lord your God will bless you in the land he is giving you" (Deuteronomy 28:8).

Working Hard

One of the best ways to be fruitful is to work hard at what you do. No matter what occupation you currently have in life—student, executive, professional, homemaker—hard work is made of three key elements: **planning**, **focus** and **perseverance**. If you remove any one of these, you will end up wasting your time. Hard work without planning leads to double work. Planned work without focus leads to waste. And if you don't persevere and pursue your goal with endurance, you might as well not have started the project in the first place! Consider what Proverbs says about each:

Planning

- **"Every prudent man acts out of knowledge, but a fool exposes his folly" (13:16).**
- **"The wisdom of the prudent is to give thought to their ways, but the folly of fools is deception" (14:8).**
- **"It is not good to have zeal without knowledge, nor to be hasty and miss the way" (19:2).**
- **"The plans of the diligent lead to profit as surely as haste leads to poverty" (21:5).**

Planning occurs when we take time before *doing* the work to *plan* the work so it can be done correctly and efficiently. Planning is where we apply the carpenter's rule: measure twice; cut only once. We honor God by *intentionally and deliberately* going about the work to which He has called us. Sometimes this means getting up a little earlier; sometimes it means working late.

A leader goes before the people to be a faithful steward of the planning process. This honors the time of the followers by making sure their work is done effectively and efficiently. Perhaps the best example of this was shown by Nehemiah. The walls around Jerusalem were broken down, and he had received permission from the king of Babylon to rebuild them. Before he or anyone else fitted a single stone to the new wall, he surveyed the work to be done, and he did this quietly, prayerfully and deliberately.

> I set out during the night with a few men. I had not told anyone what my God had put in my heart to do for Jerusalem. There were no mounts with me except the one I was riding on. By night I went out through the Valley Gate… examining the walls of Jerusalem, which had been broken down, and its gates, which had been destroyed by fire. Then I moved on toward the Fountain Gate and the King's Pool, but there was not enough room for my mount to get through; so I went up the valley by night, examining the wall. Finally, I turned back and reentered through the Valley Gate. The officials did not know where I had gone or what I was doing, because as yet *I had said nothing to the Jews or the priests or nobles or officials or any others who would be doing the work* (Nehemiah 2:12-16).

Nehemiah did this planning work quietly and unannounced. He did it with only a few men and limited resources. Docs this apply to a current situation you're in? Is there a project, an endeavor or a plan that needs this type of attention from you?

Focus

- **"He who works his land will have abundant food, but he who chases fantasies lacks judgment" (12:11).**
- **"All hard work brings a profit, but mere talk leads only to poverty" (14:23).**

Focus makes all the difference. It's the factor that converts your plans and perseverance into a *successful outcome*. Take for instance a floodlight which casts light over a wide area. The same energy source used for a floodlight can be channeled into a laser beam that is capable of cutting through steel. That's how "focus" works.

I've seen many people with get-rich-quick schemes crash and burn. The people who avoid these useless pursuits and build successful careers are those who make *daily decisions* to focus and work hard at tried, proven, legitimate business ventures. While there is a time to innovate and try new things—Proverbs is just saying we should refuse to chase fantasies and fleeting ideas. Every once in a while someone stumbles into something that becomes highly successful, but the other ninety-nine percent of us need to "keep our nose to the grindstone" consistently to bring financial success to our lives. Life has a strange way of bringing *opportunity* to the *prepared*.

Consider the truth in the proverb above—*all* hard work brings profit (not some, but *all*). Even if we don't reap immediate rewards from a project we worked on, *profit will find a way to the hard-working person*. Consider also the concept of working *your* land to have *abundant* food. What is the land God is giving you? What are the talents you have, the skills you've developed and the opportunities God has provided to match them? Work hard at these, and the Bible promises *abundant* provision.

Perseverance

- **"Lazy hands make a man poor, but diligent hands bring wealth" (10:4).**
- **"Diligent hands will rule, but laziness ends in slave labor" (12:24).**
- **"A sluggard does not plow in season; so at harvest time he looks but finds nothing" (20:4).**
- **"Do not love sleep or you will grow poor; stay awake and you will have food to spare" (20:13).**
- **"She gets up while it is still dark; she provides food for her family and portions for her servant girls. She**

considers a field and buys it; out of her earnings she plants a vineyard. She sets about her work vigorously; her arms are strong for her tasks. She sees that her trading is profitable, and her lamp does not go out at night" (31:15-18).

Perseverance is the hard part. That's when we punch through the difficult times by *sheer force of will*—relying on God's promise: "I can do all things through Christ who strengthens me" (Philippians 4:13). Pushing happens when we work *even when we don't want to*. This means getting out of bed when you don't want to and putting in another day—even after all the inspiration and enthusiasm are gone. My mother would frequently refer to perseverance as "stick-to-it-ive-ness."

Working hard is actually the easy way of doing work because it takes less effort than being lazy *in the long run*. By "putting your elbows into it," rather than slowly mushing your way through the day's work, you will get your work done much faster and more thoroughly, leaving more time for rest and recuperation. The Lord knows what your best looks like, and *He wants all of it*.

.

Being a Good Steward
of Our Possessions

Proverbs:

- "The lazy man does not roast his game, but the diligent man prizes his possessions" (12:27).
- "Of what use is money in the hand of a fool, since he has no desire to get wisdom?" (17:16).

We should respect God by taking care of what He gives us! Why is this important? There are many reasons. Let's consider three of them:

First, how we handle our possessions is a good indication of our spiritual character. Don't get me wrong here—the Lord would not have us spit-shining our possessions all day and ignoring the *true* treasures of this world, which are our relationships with people. The concept here is simple: how we take care of our stuff is an indication of our character. It's not about taking care of things so they will last forever, because they won't. Rather it's all about *demonstrating responsibility to the Lord*—taking good care of our possessions is just one way we do this.

Second, if we want more in the future, we need to be faithful with what He has given us now. If we want to be entrusted with more from the Lord, we need to be a faithful caretaker—a steward—of what He has given us already. Have you ever noticed others saying, "If I had this or that I would take great care of it." Or, "If I had that job or this job I would do incredibly well!" The question is, how are those people taking care of the resources the Lord has already entrusted to them? Only after we have demonstrated faithfulness with what we have—our obligations and our possessions—can we be entrusted with more valuable things. Christ spoke on this in Luke 16:10-12.

> Whoever can be trusted with very little can also be trusted with much, and whoever is dishonest with very little will also be dishonest with much. So if you have not been trustworthy in handling worldly wealth, who will trust you with true riches? And if you have not been trustworthy with someone else's property, who will give you property of your own?

This is a spiritual principle—a law if you will. He who is faithful with little can, *and will*, be trusted with much.

Third, being a faithful steward preserves our God-given assets and resources and allows God to do even more with them. Spending a small amount of money two or three times a year to change your engine oil can double the "life expectancy" of your car. Spending the same amount on a gym membership can prolong your life by an additional ten to fifteen years (that is, if you *use* the membership!). Yes, stewardship counts for our bodies too, because our bodies are just another possession God has temporarily entrusted to us.

Just how do these principles of being a faithful steward play out in our lives? Here are some other practical examples.

- Have you ever heard the statement, "You get what you pay for?" It's true. Not always, or under every situation, but generally you will find this to be a true statement. Spending a little extra to buy better quality items will save you time and money in the future by not having to replace the item later.
- When it comes to spending "big money," most of the time it pays off to get three bids. This allows you to be an informed shopper as you learn from the different experts,

and the competitive process usually works as an incentive for bidders to keep their prices reasonable.

- Research the key facts, not just some of the facts, before making a significant purchase. It only takes a little time to save a lot of money in the long run. In fact, sometimes taking just that extra ten or twenty minutes of research can save thousands of dollars and a lot of time over the long run. The internet is an incredibly friendly and efficient way to do this.

I will never forget moving into our home eight years ago. While some friends were helping us move in, my friend Rob said, "Wow! God sure has blessed you with a nice home and some neat things—I bet the only reason He did is because He knows that neither will distract you from Him." By God's grace I had reached a place in my spiritual growth where this was true. All things in this world are passing away (Matthew 6:19), but the character we develop while learning how to be a faithful steward of them is eternal.

Consistently Spending Less than Your Cash Flow and Avoiding Excessive Debt

Proverbs:

- "He who loves pleasure will become poor; whoever loves wine and oil will never be rich" (21:17).
- "The rich rule over the poor, and the borrower is servant to the lender" (22:7)
- "Do not be a man who strikes hands in pledge or puts up security for debts; if you lack the means to pay, your very bed will be snatched from under you" (22:26-27).

Remember this: every time you spend money, you're ultimately making a *spiritual* decision. Spending less than you make and doing this consistently over a lifetime will allow God's financial best for your life. We can demonstrate faithfulness and wisdom in our lives by carefully managing how much we spend and what we buy and by avoiding consumer debt.

We live in a debt-laden society. Credit opportunities flood the mailboxes of young people after leaving home, and many become trapped in debt at very young ages. After starting with just a small level of consumer debt, sometimes we become "overrun" with more debt than our cash flow can handle. Soon our outgoing money quickly exceeds our income. This leads to bondage, as Proverbs reminds us: "The rich rule over the poor, and the borrower is servant to the lender" (Proverbs 22:7). It only takes practice and discipline to spend less than you make, and doing this consistently over a lifetime will lead to blessings and ultimately trust from God to provide us with greater resources (see Luke 16:10-12).

God provides us with resources for our *balanced enjoyment* (for example, 1 Timothy 6:6-8, Psalm 104:15), but not for our *fulfillment*. God wants us to find fulfillment *in Him*. Notice how Proverbs 21:17 uses the term "love" twice: "He who **loves** pleasure will become poor; whoever **loves** wine and oil will never be rich." One commentator remarks that this type of love (that is, which is essentially being obsessed with or seeking fulfillment through material things) is "a reversal of priorities" and advises, "One who seeks justice and virtue will also find life's enjoyments, but one who puts those ahead of virtue will end up missing them both" (Koptak, 2003, p. 503). Christ offers the purest perspective on material versus eternal things.

> Therefore I tell you, do not worry about your life, what you will eat or drink; or about your body, what you will wear. Is not life more important than food, and the body more important than clothes? Look at the birds of the air; they do not sow or reap or store away in barns, and yet your heavenly Father feeds them. Are you not much more valuable than they? Who of you by worrying can add a single hour to his life? And why do you worry about clothes? See how the lilies of the field grow. They do not labor or spin. Yet I tell you that not even Solomon in all his splendor was dressed like one of these. If that is how God clothes the grass of the field, which is here today and tomorrow is thrown into the fire, will he not much more clothe you, O you of little faith? So do not worry, saying, "What shall we eat?" or "What shall we drink?" or "What shall we wear?" For the pagans run after all these things, and your heavenly Father knows that you need them. But seek first his kingdom and his righteousness, and all these things will be given to you as well (Matthew 6:25-33).

The Lord's instruction in this passage is clear: we should put our focus first on Him and His kingdom; the rest will fall into place.

Christ also said in this passage that we should not be obsessed with this world and all its fleeting and often distracting resources. The apostle Paul also reminds us of the importance of having such a focus: "Set your minds on things above, not on earthly things. For you died, and your life is now hidden with Christ in God" (Colossians 3:2-3).

I have found that our kind Lord often regulates our finances purposefully and deliberately because He knows the true nature of our (sometimes deceitful) hearts (see Jeremiah 17:9-10). As our loving father, He knows it is in our own best interest to be balanced in this area: "Keep falsehood and lies far from me; give me neither poverty nor riches, but give me only my daily bread. Otherwise, I may have too much and disown you and say, 'Who is the Lord?' Or I may become poor and steal, and so dishonor the name of my God" (30:8-9).

We tend to turn away from Him when we feel we don't need Him anymore for our daily subsistence. Moses predicted God's people would leave Him when their resources were abundant.

> When you have eaten and are satisfied, praise the Lord your God for the good land he has given you. Be careful that you do not forget the Lord your God, failing to observe his commands, his laws and his decrees that I am giving you this day. Otherwise, when you eat and are satisfied, when you build fine houses and settle down, and when your herds and flocks grow large and your silver and gold increase and all you have is multiplied, then your heart will become proud and you will forget the Lord your God, who brought you out of Egypt, out of the land of slavery (Deuteronomy 8:10-14, see also Deuteronomy 31:20).

Spending less than we earn and avoiding excessive debt are sure ways to live within the means the Lord has carved out for each one of us. May we seek balance in our lives in this area, for "godliness with contentment is great gain. . .we brought nothing into the world, and we can take nothing out of it. But if we have food and clothing, we will be content with that" (1 Timothy 6:6-8).

Saving Consistently, Little by Little, with a Long-Term Perspective

Proverbs:

- "Go to the ant, you sluggard; consider its ways and be wise! It has no commander, no overseer or ruler, yet it stores its provisions in summer and gathers its food at harvest" (6:6-8).
- "Dishonest money dwindles away, but he who gathers money little by little makes it grow" (13:11).
- "He who works his land will have abundant food, but the one who chases fantasies will have his fill of poverty. A faithful man will be richly blessed, but one eager to get rich will not go unpunished" (28:19-20).
- "Ants are creatures of little strength, yet they store up their food in the summer" (30:25).

God's message about saving is so simple He uses ants to deliver it! If you want to amass wealth, stay away from get-rich-quick schemes and develop a *pattern* and *habit* of consistently saving money in *reasonably conservative* and *diversified* investments. Consider what is meant by a person who "*works his land*" (Proverbs 28:19) and being a *faithful* person who will be richly blessed (Proverbs 28:20). God expects us to labor in the field He has called us to and to do this faithfully to be blessed. When a farmer puts fifteen corn seeds into the ground, he expects to get fifteen corn plants, with each yielding several ears of corn. When you work your land—when you plant your seeds—take some of what you earn and save it. Then let it grow as a farmer grows his crops—patiently without digging it up before it's ripe! See also Proverbs 20:21, 21:20 and 13:22.

Albert Einstein referred to compound interest as "the greatest mathematical discovery of all time." Consider the following example involving twin brothers, Patrick and Frank, who were born on the same day. When they were both twenty, they began work at the same company in the same job, earning the exact same salary every year. In fact, they both stayed in these jobs for the next forty years and shared the same retirement party when they turned sixty-five.

While they were young, they had very different spending habits. Patrick was the more diligent of the two and decided to immediately open a retirement savings account when he started work the first day. Every year he contributed just $2,000 into his account. For the next forty-five years (until he was sixty-five), regardless of the financial ups and downs he encountered in his life, he never failed to invest the $2,000 every year. During some years he never felt the money leaving his income stream. During other years it was a struggle, but nonetheless he put his $2,000 in the bank each and every year. Due to the magic of compounding interest (even when his investment was made in a conservative retirement account earning six percent per year), Patrick's consistent $2,000/year investment earned him a whopping sum of $500,000—enough for him and his wife to retire comfortably. He only put in $90,000 of his own money ($2,000 per year for forty-five years)—the rest was earned by the wonder of compound interest.

Now let's turn to Patrick's twin brother, Frank. Frank enjoyed spending his money on quickly depreciating things like fancy cars and other grown-up toys. Fifteen years later, at age thirty-five, he finally woke up and decided to start saving for his future. So, for the next thirty years (until he reached age sixty-five), he piled $3,000 per year into his retirement fund—thinking that investing $1,000 more than his brother's $2,000 per year would allow him to catch up. His retirement investment also earned a modest six percent interest, and he let his money grow without taking out a cent until he turned sixty-five exactly. Even though Frank managed to invest fifty percent more per year than his brother Patrick ($3,000 per year versus $2,000 per year), he only had $175,000 when he retired at age sixty-five.

The lesson from this story is simple: you can either work for money or let your money work for you. Patrick and Frank each invested the same total amount ($90,000) into their retirement savings. Patrick invested $2,000 per year for forty-five years; Frank put in $3,000 per year for thirty years. Yet they ended up with vastly different retirement "nest eggs"—Patrick with $500,000 and Frank with $175,000. Patrick ended up with nearly three times the amount Frank did—*all for starting a mere fifteen years earlier with his investment savings.*

If ants can save, little-by-little, over a long period of time, we can too. "Go to the ant, you sluggard; consider its ways and be wise! It has no commander, no overseer or ruler, yet it stores its provisions in summer and gathers its food at harvest" (Proverbs 6:6-8).

Should Patrick enjoy his retirement wealth lavishly? While some indulgences are nice, consider how he can now be freed for serving the kingdom. There's also something to be said for leaving an inheritance to those who follow after us. In fact, if you have the resources, set up financial trusts that will carry your desires and intentions for your family for many years after you're gone. Trusts will have stability and momentum that will far outlive you, your spouse and even your own children. Proverbs 13:22 beckons, "A good man leaves an inheritance for his children's children, but a sinner's wealth is stored up for the righteous."

Pillar 6: Impartial

The Greek term used for the impartial wisdom pillar in James 3:17 is *adiakritos,* which means "undistinguished, being without dubiousness, ambiguity or uncertainty; and free from prejudice." This term is used only once in the entire New Testament, so James wasn't being random when he selected this word to represent one of the key pillars of wisdom.

Being impartial supports and weaves together a well rounded house of wisdom. Impartiality is critical to the infrastructure of wisdom's house because of its *supportive* role. Imagine a completely humble and submissive person who is not impartial. How far will their humility carry them in life before their failure to be impartial tangles up their life? Consider a person who loves mercy but is partial to only certain types of people. Surely their lack of impartiality will quickly ruin their efforts in practicing mercy.

Being impartial is especially important when you're placed in any type of leadership role—ranging from a project leader, older sibling or parent to business executive. Leaders who are not impartial—even in the small things—can quickly destroy the trust their followers place in them. Solomon (who wrote most of Proverbs) had an incredibly wise leader for a father—King David himself. I'm sure he paid attention to his dad's example on how to live a life directed by wisdom, including the importance of being impartial.

An example of impartiality occurred when David led an army of six hundred warriors on a journey to recapture their wives and children who had been taken captive by their enemies. While hot on the tracks of their enemies, they came to a ravine where two hundred men stayed behind because they were too exhausted to cross. David and his four hundred men pursued and eventually returned with every single captive—completely unharmed. They even reclaimed all of the supplies stolen from them and some "extra" supplies from their fallen enemies.

During their victory march home they met up with the two hundred men who had stayed behind. Some of David's followers said, "Because they did not go out with us, we will not share with them the plunder we recovered. However, each man may take his wife and children and go" (1 Samuel 30:22). To this David replied, "No, my brothers, you must not do that with what the Lord has given us. He has protected us and handed over to us the forces that came against us. Who will listen to what you say? The share of the man who stayed with the supplies is to be the same as that of him who went down to the battle. All will share alike" (30:23-24).

This story concludes by stating that "David made this a statute and ordinance for Israel from that day to this" (1 Samuel 30:25). In this way, the importance of being impartial as a leader has been permanently recorded into God's Scripture. Solomon continued during his life's journey to record the importance of being impartial in the riches of his proverbs.

Balancing Mercy and Justice

Proverbs:

- "Acquitting the guilty and condemning the innocent — the Lord detests them both" (17:15).
- "It is not good to be partial to the wicked or to deprive the innocent of justice" (18:5).
- "A hot-tempered man must pay the penalty; if you rescue him, you will have to do it again" (19:19).
- "These also are sayings of the wise: To show partiality in judging is not good: Whoever says to the guilty, 'You are innocent' — peoples will curse him and nations denounce him. But it will go well with those who convict the guilty, and rich blessing will come upon them" (24:23-25).

Have you ever let someone "off the hook" only to regret it later? Consider circumstances involving a child, a friend or someone you've supervised at work. Have there been times when you should have disciplined someone but chose to have mercy instead?

Certainly showing grace and mercy is an appropriate response in many circumstances where a person's behaviors are deserving of punishment. *But sometimes it's not the best choice.* Consider a small fire that starts in your kitchen trash can. One way to put out the fire is simply to move the can into a closet and shut the door. Sometimes this will extinguish the fire because it removes the oxygen supply.

Perhaps ninety-nine times out of a hundred this will work. But one time in a hundred it won't, and the fire will grow to consume your entire house.

This is similar to disciplining children or admonishing friends or co-workers whom God places under our care. If the person stumbles in some way but has a *truly repentant heart* and will not likely repeat the same behavior in the future, *sparing discipline* may be the appropriate choice. On the other hand, the person needs to fully experience the consequences of their choices so they can grow and change, and if we bail them out of trouble we will need to do it over and over again, as Proverbs 19:19 instructs: "A hot-tempered man must pay the penalty; if you rescue him, you will have to do it again."

When I was fifteen I had a major quarrel with my dad. Words and threats were exchanged, and I ran away from home, only to return later that night and "borrow" his car for a rebellious joy ride with a few equally defiant friends. It wasn't long before our amateur driving skills drew the attention of a patrol officer, and we were pulled over and brought to a restaurant where our parents were called to retrieve us. When I was face-to-face with the *natural consequences* that were about to befall me (a night in the juvenile detention center), my attitude was immediately changed. My crooked character straightened like an arrow while I sat at the table listening to my parents deliberate with the officers about what to do with this "mischievous teenager." My repentant attitude made it evident to them that I was ripe for grace. That night grace was offered as I was released to return home. I grew from this experience and never again repeated such behavior. This is an example of when grace *was* the appropriate choice. I had a repentant heart that others could sense was true and sincere, and they knew further consequences were unnecessary. My heart was changed, and everyone knew it.

But what about circumstances where grace is *not* the most effective choice? Consider this story a friend recently shared about an experience he had while working as a police officer in a remote town twenty years ago. One night while on patrol he pulled over a person who was driving erratically. After investigating this person's condition a little further, it became clear he was only *slightly* under the influence. He wasn't completely drunk, but it was obvious he had just "one drink too many." After learning the man seemed to be a decent, hard-working citizen who happened to live only a few more miles down the road, my friend let him go with just a verbal warning. In doing so, he offered this tipsy, but not completely drunk, driver mercy and grace, *but not justice.*

Two weeks later this same man was driving home from the same bar—again after having "just one too many" drinks. But on this trip home he had a head-on collision with an oncoming car that killed the unsuspecting driver. Clearly in this case my friend's choice of letting the person "off the hook" and extending mercy was *not* the best decision. If he would have allowed the full weight of the law (a drunk driving arrest) to impact this person's life, the death of the innocent victim might have been prevented.

How can you know when to respond to a situation with mercy and grace or with justice and discipline? We can do this by viewing the situation in the same way God views us when we sin—by looking at our repentance, our remorse and our willingness to turn around. Maturity and discernment are necessary to know which is the appropriate choice.

Reflect

"Do not pervert justice; do not show partiality to the poor or favoritism to the great, but judge your neighbor fairly" (Leviticus 19:15).

Sowing and Reaping

Proverbs:

- "Wisdom calls aloud in the street, she raises her voice in the public squares; at the head of the noisy streets she cries out; in the gateways of the city she makes her speech: 'How long will you simple ones love your simple ways? How long will mockers delight in mockery and fools hate knowledge? If you had responded to my rebuke, I would have poured out my heart to you and made my thoughts known to you. But since you rejected me when I called and no one gave heed when I stretched out my hand, since you ignored all my advice and would not accept my rebuke, I in turn will laugh at your disaster; I will mock when calamity overtakes you—when calamity overtakes you like a storm, when disaster sweeps over you like a whirlwind, when distress and trouble overwhelm you. Then they will call to me but I will not answer; they will look for me but will not find me. Since they hated knowledge and did not choose to fear the Lord, since they would not accept my advice and spurned my rebuke, they will eat the fruit of their ways and be filled with the fruit of their schemes. For the waywardness of the simple will kill them, and the complacency of fools will destroy them; but whoever listens to me will live in safety and be at ease, without fear of harm'" (1:20-1:33).

- **"A man's own folly ruins his life, yet his heart rages against the Lord" (19:3).**

Proverbs 1:20-33 makes it clear that godly wisdom doesn't play favorites between people. If you practice the principles of wisdom, you will be blessed in many ways (see examples in the table below). If you don't, you won't. Don't get me wrong—we all know bad things happen to good people. But people who choose to live by wisdom's principles will spare themselves the "extra" bad things that others who don't live by these principles will bring on themselves!

Wisdom stands by, waiting and hoping people will choose her way: "If you had responded to my rebuke, I would have poured out my heart to you and made my thoughts known to you." Like love, wisdom is not forceful or demanding of its own way. Wisdom can, and will, wait. But to those who choose to continue in their sinful ways, the seeds they plant will eventually grow up into a future harvest. There is no cheating this process. Oftentimes, when these sinful actions are sown into the soil of one's life and later harvested, people rage at God as if He had something to do with it ("A man's own folly ruins his life, yet his heart rages against the Lord," Proverbs 19:3). While these principles are difficult to digest, this is exactly what God's Word teaches in Proverbs and other Scriptures.

Do not be deceived: God cannot be mocked. A man reaps what he sows. The one who sows to please his sinful nature, from that nature will reap destruction; the one who sows to please the Spirit, from the Spirit will reap eternal life. Let us not become weary in doing good, for at the proper time we will reap a harvest if we do not give up (Galatians 6:7-9).

The table below shows the consequences for choosing wisdom—or not.

Proverbs	Consequences of Rejecting or Choosing Wisdom	
	Rejecting *or* Neglecting Wisdom	Choosing Wisdom
1:20-33	Self-destructive lifestyle	Self-preservation and safety
2:7-8	Failure	Victory and protection
3:5-6	Confusion and ineffectiveness	Direction and purpose
3:13-15; 10:22	Emptiness and void; or financial resources without contentment	Wealth that money cannot offer; sufficient financial resources for our life's calling
3:16-18	Discontentment, dissatisfaction	Long life, peace and blessing
3:21-3:26; 28:14	Sudden disaster, ruin and setbacks	Safety, security, restfulness
3:33	Cursing	Blessing
3:35	Shame	Honor
8:32-34	Harm	God's favor
12:7	Insecurity and instability	Firm standing and security
12:12; 14:11; 16:20	Loss	Fruitfulness and blessing
12:21	Trouble	Security
20:7	Fleeting life	Multi-generational blessing

Sometimes making the decision to choose wisdom doesn't yield immediate results. But it *always* pays off in the long run.

Workplace Fairness

Proverbs:

- "The Lord abhors dishonest scales, but accurate weights are his delight" (11:1).
- "Honest scales and balances are from the Lord; all the weights in the bag are of his making" (16:11).
- "Differing weights and differing measures—the Lord detests them both" (20:10).
- "The Lord detests differing weights, and dishonest scales do not please him" (20:23).

Have you seen someone be promoted over others who were more qualified than they were for the position? Someone receive a job for which they were not qualified? When this happens, at least three major problems are created.

First, feelings of shame can emerge for the undeserving person who received the promotion. They can also develop arrogance and pride when moved to positions of responsibility for which they are not qualified. They can become ostracized and alienated by their co-workers and peers. They lose self-respect and the veneration of their co-workers because they know others more qualified were overlooked for the position.

Second, the reputation of the company can suffer, and the management staff can lose the respect of their employees and potential employees. "They don't pay attention to job requirements...it's all about 'who you know' or some other characteristic that will get you hired or promoted here" are discussions in the workplace and applicant population that taint the company's reputation.

Third, the applicants who competed for the open positions and/ or employees who were overlooked for promotional opportunities can become disheartened. Unsuccessful applicants complain: "This company does not care about our skills or qualifications—it's all about politics, connections or some other factor that will get you a job." Employees who are overlooked for promotions can become resigned or even belligerent thinking, "Why even try to perform increasingly better on my job if management will not reward me with career advancement?"

Management and employers can prevent or alleviate these three problems by following these practices: (1) openly posting career paths so that employees know how to advance in the company; (2) accurately and objectively assessing job qualifications; and (3) openly disclosing and disseminating the job requirements for hiring or promotional opportunities. If God has entrusted you with opening or closing the gate for career opportunities, you need to be responsible about it, and the advice presented above can help.

I've worked in the field of equal employment opportunity (EEO) consulting for nearly two decades. Throughout my career I've watched the political atmosphere shift between liberal and conservative several times. As these climates change, proponents on both extremes typically maintain their positions.

Some affirmative action and social justice advocates believe the *past* societal ills of oppression, discrimination or segregation justify requiring individual employers to adopt *current* personnel policies that directly favor the impacted groups at some level. That is, the past sins of *society in general* demand that each individual employer change their *current* personnel practices in ways that are tailored to specific groups of people, rather than based solely on job requirements.

Some conservative advocates hold the position that, regardless of historical discrimination or the present conduct of other employers, each job seeker should freely compete in the marketplace and be hired strictly in order of relevant qualifications. Under this viewpoint individual employers are not required to make any adjustments to account for the general past societal ills or the sins of other employers in their industry or region.

For years these two extremes have waged war in social settings, courtrooms, academia and the media. So which side's viewpoints are more valid? Does God align Himself more on the conservative or the liberal side? Actually, God's not on either one. God does not reside in the heavenly realm aligning Himself with the political parties of this world. But a balanced reading of the Scriptures will show any humble student that God hates oppression and discrimination (for example, Isaiah 58); has an incredible heart for the poor, the oppressed and the voiceless (for example, the vast majority of Christ's ministries were targeted to these groups); and simultaneously is a supporter of enterprising, hard-working individuals who build wealth and opportunity for others (for example, Proverbs 6:6-11, 20:4, 24:30-34). God has no desire for people to amass enormous wealth and opportunities just to hoard them and not share with others in need (for example, 1 Timothy 6:17-18, Acts 5:1-5).

The four proverbs above make it abundantly clear that God condemns unequal or inaccurate weights and balances, which can be illustrated in this current discussion as misrepresenting job requirements in ways that understate *or* exaggerate the actual job requirements. This is one of the primary goals of human resource professionals: to use a balanced scale to weigh applicant qualifications on one side and job requirements on the other. In this way, the biblical analogy fits perfectly.

What a challenge this presents to all professionals who work in some type of management role! When struggling to apply these principles in my own career, I brought up these issues with my pastor who shared with me some incredibly wise words: "If your practices have managed to make both extreme sides of the civil rights continuum upset at you, then you've probably done a good job." Extreme forms of affirmative action result in tokenism and hazing for the group it benefits and deep feelings of resentment and inequity for the group it doesn't. Extreme conservatism results in disadvantaged groups being left out of employment opportunities and the middle class and ultimately leads to the employer developing a reputation in society that hurts the financial bottom line. Proverbs cautions that hiring practices should focus primarily on the true requirements of the job: "Like an archer who wounds at random is he who hires a fool or any passer-by" (26:10). God also prohibits favoritism (James 2), which suggests that applicants should be offered only positions for which they are clearly qualified—no matter who the applicant is.

God's Conditional Blessing: Why Do Some People's Lives Appear to Be More Blessed than Others?

Proverbs:

- "Blessed is the man who finds wisdom, the man who gains understanding, for she is more profitable than silver and yields better returns than gold. She is more precious than rubies; nothing you desire can compare with her. Long life is in her right hand; in her left hand are riches and honor" (3:13-16).
- "The blessing of the Lord brings wealth, and he adds no trouble to it" (10:22).
- "The wicked desire the plunder of evil men, but the root of the righteous flourishes" (12:12).
- "Misfortune pursues the sinner, but prosperity is the reward of the righteous. A good man leaves an inheritance for his children's children, but a sinner's wealth is stored up for the righteous" (13:21-22).
- "The house of the wicked will be destroyed, but the tent of the upright will flourish" (14:11).

A person who pursues godliness will practice impartiality, for God in His infinite wisdom is impartial to His own people. For example, those who choose to live by wisdom's principles and standards will be rewarded with both material and spiritual blessings, and those who don't will not (see proverbs above). Even if the lives of those who reject biblical wisdom appear to be richly blessed, Proverbs forecasts this will only be a temporary condition: "Cast but a glance at riches, and they are gone, for they will surely sprout wings and fly off to the sky like an eagle" (23:5), and "A good man leaves an inheritance for his children's children, but a sinner's wealth is stored up for the righteous" (13:22).

The extent to which we choose to apply God's wisdom principles in our lives correlates (in many respects) to how we will be blessed. Discussing how people receive blessings from God and why some people receive more than others is a dangerous topic. It is very easily misunderstood and has been the cause of raging theological debates for centuries. Most recently in this century some teachers have ventured into prosperity theology which asserts that Christians need to use spiritual faith to claim financial blessings. This "name it and claim it" teaching states that the only reason some have financial blessings and others don't is the result of having faith or not.

While this extra-biblical teaching is farfetched, there is *some* truth behind the notion that our faith translates into actions that will in fact lead to spiritual and (in many cases) material blessings. This is because having faith that God really exists will lead us to govern our lives after the wisdom principles found in Scripture, which will in fact bring God's blessings into our lives. Further, God requires faith if we are to please Him ("And without faith it is impossible to please God, because anyone who comes to him must believe that he exists and that he rewards those who earnestly seek him," Hebrews 11:6).

If God loves all of His children equally, then why does it sometimes appear that He blesses some of His children more than others? Let's face it—we've all been envious of others at times. We've all attended church on occasions and thought, *Why did he get that job, and I'm stuck with mine?* or *How can they can afford that car, and I'm driving this cheap one?*

Consider two people who were born at the same socio-economic level. Further assume they were born with the same talents, financial resources and opportunities. Let's say only one of them seeks God and applies the principles of scriptural wisdom in her life. She gives generously of her time, talents and treasure to God and does this for years. Then assume the other person is rebellious toward God and resists God's calling and purpose for their lives in every area. Rather than putting God first, he holds back his life and talents and becomes self-consumed with his own selfish pursuits in life. To him, God is somewhere on the proverbial "back burner."

Which person do you think God will bless more? Perhaps a better question is, "Which person *can* God bless more?" The first person evoked the spiritual principles of God's blessing in their lives. By putting God and His wisdom principles as top priorities, she *positioned her life to be blessed by God*. God loves His children, and He wants to bless us all (James 1:17); but sometimes we allow our lives to get off track in certain areas, and He cannot bless us. This principle reminds me of a saying, "If you don't feel close to God, who moved?" Just as we can't go on a ride at an amusement park without first waiting in line, we must first wait on God to enjoy His best for our lives and stay fast in His ways.

> Let us not become weary in doing good, for at the proper time we will reap a harvest *if we do not give up*. Therefore, as we have opportunity, let us do good to all people, especially to those who belong to the family of believers (Galatians 6:9-10).

Am I saying God will financially bless the socks off believers who apply these principles? No, but I am saying God will bless your life (in many ways, not just financially) more than you personally would have been blessed had you not placed yourself in a position to receive God's best for *your life*.

A spiritually wise friend and I were discussing this very issue once, and he asked me, "Do you think that if I did anything different in life I would gain more material wealth?" He was on a career track to become a high school teacher which was exactly what God had desired for him. He was experiencing God's very best for him and, while this did not include a six-figure income, he was on course to receive God's very best for *his life*, which is better than any worldly riches could ever offer. His life was already blessed to the fullest, even though his modest teacher salary was all he could reasonably expect for years to come. This was *plenty* for the life to which God had called him. As the apostle Paul said, "But godliness with contentment is great gain. For we brought nothing into the world, and we can take nothing out of it. But if we have food and clothing, we will be content with that" (1 Timothy 6:6-8).

Discipline and Natural Consequences

Proverbs:

- "He who spares the rod hates his son, but he who loves him is careful to discipline him" (13:24).
- "Discipline your son, for in that there is hope; do not be a willing party to his death" (19:18).
- "Even a child is known by his actions, by whether his conduct is pure and right" (20:11).
- "Train a child in the way he should go, and when he is old he will not turn from it" (22:6).
- "These also are sayings of the wise: To show partiality in judging is not good: Whoever says to the guilty, 'You are innocent'—peoples will curse him and nations denounce him. But it will go well with those who convict the guilty, and rich blessing will come upon them" (24:23-26).
- "Discipline your son, and he will give you peace; he will bring delight to your soul" (29:17).

Some parents discipline their children by raising their voices, making idle threats or stooping to their child's level and arguing. We've all seen parents with children in grocery stores where the child, and not the parent, was in charge. In such situations it seems as if children are raising children. A more effective way of parenting older children is to calmly and clearly lay out the "code of conduct" or desired outcomes (homework completed, chores done before dinner, room cleaned and so on), along with very clear consequences that will be *consistently enforced* based on their completion or incompletion. In fact, it is sometimes better not to discipline children than to enforce consequences only randomly! Setting up clear expectations that have natural consequences allows the parent to enjoy the benefits of being impartial because the parent is set apart from the "sting" of discipline. The child perceives their own actions as the trigger for the discipline, rather than the parent's actions.

God is much the same way when it comes to discipline and natural consequences. Oftentimes—for our own good and character development—God does not serve as a buffer between us and the natural consequences we deserve. The natural consequences of overeating and under-exercising are lethargy, excess weight gain and sometimes disease. The natural consequences of raising unruly kids are embarrassment and difficulties when they get older (for both the children and parents). The natural consequence of filling one's mind with garbage on TV is having a mind that is drawn to the things of the world, rather than to the better things God has for our lives.

God does not stand by and yell at His children and occasionally and randomly whip out punishments every third time we do something wrong. The Bible is very clear, however, that God does in fact discipline His children.

> Endure hardship as discipline; God is treating you as sons. For what son is not disciplined by his father? If you are not disciplined (and everyone undergoes discipline), then you are illegitimate children and not true sons. Moreover, we have all had human fathers who disciplined us and we respected them for it. How much more should we submit to the Father of our spirits and live! Our fathers disciplined us for a little while as they thought best; but God disciplines us for our good, that we may share in his holiness. No discipline seems pleasant at the time, but painful. Later on, however, it

produces a harvest of righteousness and peace for those who have been trained by it (Hebrews 12:7-11).

When my son, Matthew, was four years old I asked him to clean up his castle blocks which he had left on the floor. After several minutes of his stalling, I asked him again but this time with a natural consequence of "clean up the blocks or they will be put away for a few days in the closet." When he still did not pick up the blocks he earned the natural consequences of having them put into the closet. In this situation, rather than seeing his dad as the mean perpetrator who is stealing his toys, he saw that my response to his poor choice was "I'm sorry you chose that behavior; I hope you make a better choice next time." There was no raised blood pressure, no yelling and no resentment, and he was able to make a connection between his own choices and actions rather than perceiving his dad as just being a "mean disciplinarian."

This is exactly what is meant by the proverb, "He who spares the rod hates his son, but he who loves him is careful to discipline him" (13:24). "Sparing the rod" means to act as a buffer between your child and "what he has coming to him." Practicing impartiality by laying down the consequences that are related to certain behaviors (or the lack thereof) is a much wiser choice. Discipline like this will enable your children to "give you peace" and "bring delight to your soul" (29:17).

Pillar 7: Sincere

The Greek term used for the sincere wisdom pillar in James 3:17 is *anupokrits*, which means "unfeigned, undisguised, genuine, without hypocrisy, of good character, and lacking pretense and prideful show." This wisdom pillar is central to Wisdom's house. It is a "corner pillar" that supports the entire infrastructure. Take this pillar away, and the house crashes down. Deceitfulness is at the opposite end of sincerity and is also included in the discussion in this chapter regarding what Proverbs has to say about this essential pillar.

Be Open and Honest Now—or Someone Will Be Sorry Later

Proverbs:

- "Better is open rebuke than hidden love. Wounds from a friend can be trusted, but an enemy multiplies kisses" (27:5-6).
- "He who rebukes a man will in the end gain more favor than he who has a flattering tongue" (28:23).
- "As iron sharpens iron, so one man sharpens another" (27:17).

When I was eighteen I was caught up in willful and habitual sin. We can skip the details—let's just say I was stuck in a pattern of sin and had no plans of stopping any time soon. Then my friend Rob found an opportunity to confront me. He sat down and showed me, gently but directly, that my lifestyle and choices were separating me from God. He pointed out that my sin was preventing me from receiving *God's best* for my life. I was off track, and my sin was positioning my life *outside of God's fullest blessing*. Somewhere deep down inside I knew Rob was right.

When he confronted me, I was defensive and pushed him away. But he stayed his course and continued. After just a few minutes of his calm but direct "carefrontation," he was done and then left after assuring me he would be there for me if I wanted to talk further.

While it wasn't immediate, I eventually turned around, and that conversation was part of the reason I did. God took what Rob had said and used it to convict me when I was alone and had some time to reflect. My life was destined to fail if I continued down that road, but he helped me turn around. I have never been the same since. My marriage, our children, our business—these blessings would *not exist* today unless I had taken a 180-degree turn away from sin and toward God.

When God brings someone into our lives that we should confront, but don't, we're not being sincere or honest with them because true godly sincerity happens when our internal perspectives align with our external actions and words. Sometimes it's not appropriate to confront someone about their sin. There is an appropriate time and place for everything, and sometimes people are too fragile for confrontation and need love and acceptance above all else we can offer them. But sometimes God does want us to confront someone in sin: "Remember this: Whoever turns a sinner from the error of his way will save him from death and cover over a multitude of sins" (James 5:20).

At times we must be ready to wound a friend and risk a friendship, by confronting someone when we're convinced it's our time to act. In doing this, we may suffer short-term discontent in exchange for long-term favor from the person later (Proverbs 28:23). Biblical confrontation should be done gently, with sincerity and without hypocrisy. Consider these guidelines.

- "Brothers, if someone is caught in a sin, you who are spiritual should restore him gently. But watch yourself, or you also may be tempted. Carry each other's burdens, and in this way you will fulfill the law of Christ" (Galatians 6:1-2).
- "Why do you look at the speck of sawdust in your brother's eye and pay no attention to the plank in your own eye? How can you say to your brother, 'Let me take the speck out of your eye,' when all the time there is a plank in your own eye? You hypocrite, first take the plank out of

your own eye, and then you will see clearly to remove the speck from your brother's eye" (Matthew 7:3-5).

To truly express Christ's love, we must be sincere. In fact, the apostle Paul says that sincerity and true love must go hand in hand. "Love must be sincere. Hate what is evil; cling to what is good" (Romans 10:9). Yes, certainly it helps to be tactful, but *we need to pull the trigger when God puts the target opportunity before us.* Consider the passage below regarding Ezekiel being a watchman for God.

> The word of the Lord came to me: "Son of man, speak to your countrymen and say to them: 'When I bring the sword against a land, and the people of the land choose one of their men and make him their watchman, and he sees the sword coming against the land and blows the trumpet to warn the people, then if anyone hears the trumpet but does not take warning and the sword comes and takes his life, his blood will be on his own head. Since he heard the sound of the trumpet but did not take warning, his blood will be on his own head. If he had taken warning, he would have saved himself. But if the watchman sees the sword coming and does not blow the trumpet to warn the people and the sword comes and takes the life of one of them, that man will be taken away because of his sin, but I will hold the watchman accountable for his blood.' "Son of man, I have made you a watchman for the house of Israel; so hear the word I speak and give them warning from me. When I say to the wicked, 'O wicked man, you will surely die,' and you do not speak out to dissuade him from his ways, that wicked man will die for his sin, and I will hold you accountable for his blood. But if you do warn the wicked man to turn from his ways and he does not do so, he will die for his sin, but you will have saved yourself" (Ezekiel 33:1-9).

This story sums up the principle well: If it is your time and your job to be really open and honest with someone about an issue they need to hear (for their own long-term good or for the good of others), and you don't do it, you may be held accountable by God. That's quite a burden to bear. The "easy way out" of these difficult situations is to confront them *tactfully* with the truth. Ultimately you should let your concern regarding your own accountability to God govern your actions more than your fear of the person's negative response.

Live as Who You Really Are, Without Fearing Man or Lions

Proverbs:

- "Fear of man will prove to be a snare, but whoever trusts in the Lord is kept safe" (29:25).

Living a sincere life means living out your true inner self without the external governance of those who don't have the same belief systems. Said another way, don't be tricked into the foolishness of living according to how others would desire you to live. True biblical sincerity lives beyond the constraints of mankind and is manifest in your life when you live for an audience of one: God.

This means *being real*. It means living out your innermost convictions in your outermost lifestyle that is seen by others and doing so without regard for what other people will think.

The familiar story of Daniel in the lions' den is told in the sixth chapter of the book of Daniel. Daniel was one of three supervisors who presided over 120 managers of King Darius's empire. When the two other supervisors heard of the king's plan to promote Daniel as ruler over the kingdom, they started scheming to take Daniel out of the picture. Because they could find no fault in Daniel's lifestyle or work ethic, they devised a scheme to trap Daniel. Their plot was simple: get the king to set up a temporary law that would punish anyone who prayed to any god or man except the king. Punishment would mean throwing them into the lions' den.

The king bought into the plan, not knowing Daniel (whom he loved and respected) would be the first to be tried for violating the decree. Now here is the amazing part: Daniel, after he learned the new decree had been published, immediately went home to his upstairs room and prayed three times a day—exactly as he had done before the decree was passed. After his enemies caught Daniel, they took him to the king to press charges, and, sure enough, the king was forced to feed Daniel to the lions. The story ends with God saving Daniel by using an angel to "shut the mouth" of the lions and the king instead feeding the political tricksters to the lions.

Daniel blatantly disregarded man's viewpoints and laws because they were obviously opposite to God's. In fact, he had a direct and immediate defiance against these *because he lived his life by commitment and principle, rather than by circumstances and feelings*. This was possible only because he had predetermined to set God first in his life, no matter what. Daniel didn't waffle; he didn't even need to stop and contemplate—he just *acted*.

Daniel acted this way because he *really* understood something about God—something most of us are still trying to figure out. Daniel understood God is real and present with us, rather than being someone we just hope exists. Daniel believed in a God who *really is*.

When we sin we don't have a temptation problem; we have a *belief problem*. We would be much less likely to carry through with our sinful objectives if our eyes were temporarily opened to see the spiritual realm that exists beyond what we can physically see. This is why we should live a life marked with wisdom and the sincerity that comes from wisdom—because we know God is watching. Because Daniel understood God is real, this understanding gave him the wisdom to act in a way that was lockstep with this belief. Ultimately Daniel feared God more than he did the king, the king's other leaders or even the lions. May God give us all this kind of courage!

How is fearing man rather than God a trap or a snare as outlined in Proverbs 29:25? The fear of man is a trap because it can trick us into living our lives by the wrong standard. Ultimately God will judge *our* lives, and if we live our lives according to any other standard besides God's, we will be gravely disappointed on judgment day. Hubbard (1989, p. 202) states: "*Fear of man* means crediting human beings, who are not God-fearers, with the power and wisdom to guide our lives. It means turning our pivotal decisions and basic values over to them and hence walking in their ways and not God's. It means trusting them when they are not trustworthy. It is the precise opposite of what we are commanded to do in Proverbs 3:5-6." Letting people play God for us and the results of this decision cannot help but be disastrous. Dependence on the Lord and His guidance is the only safe route because it will cause you to make decisions based on long-term ramifications (that is, the judgment seat) versus short-term consequences.

Reflect

"Let those who fear the Lord say: 'His love endures forever.' In my anguish I cried to the Lord, and he answered by setting me free. The Lord is with me; I will not be afraid. What can man do to me? The Lord is with me; he is my helper. I will look in triumph on my enemies. It is better to take refuge in the Lord than to trust in man. It is better to take refuge in the Lord than to trust in princes"

(Psalm 118:4-9).

"Do not be afraid of those who kill the body but cannot kill the soul. Rather, be afraid of the One who can destroy both soul and body in hell. Are not two sparrows sold for a penny? Yet not one of them will fall to the ground apart from the will of your Father. And even the very hairs of your head are all numbered" (Matthew 10:28-30).

"I, even I, am he who comforts you. Who are you that you fear mortal men, the sons of men, who are but grass, that you forget the Lord your Maker, who stretched out the heavens and laid the foundations of the earth, that you live in constant terror every day because of the wrath of the oppressor, who is bent on destruction? For where is the wrath of the oppressor? The cowering prisoners will soon be set free; they will not die in their dungeon, nor will they lack bread. For I am the Lord your God, who churns up the sea so that its waves roar—the Lord Almighty is his name" (Isaiah 51:12-15).

Telling the Truth—Even When It Hurts

Proverbs:

- "The integrity of the upright guides them, but the unfaithful are destroyed by their duplicity" (11:3).
- "A truthful witness gives honest testimony, but a false witness tells lies" (12:17).
- "The Lord detests lying lips, but he delights in men who are truthful" (12:22).
- "A truthful witness saves lives, but a false witness is deceitful" (14:25).
- "A false witness will not go unpunished, and he who pours out lies will perish" (19:9).
- "A corrupt witness mocks at justice, and the mouth of the wicked gulps down evil" (19:28).
- "A false witness will perish, and whoever listens to him will be destroyed forever" (21:28).

Living a sincere life means accurately representing the truth. One of the more challenging aspects of my career is serving as an expert witness in court cases. When testifying in these settings, a court stenographer uses a special machine to take down every single word I say—including stutters, "hmms" and "mis-speaks." Everything is recorded on a transcript that creates a permanent record of my opinions. After a word comes out of my mouth, it's out—and there is no taking it back.

The attorneys on both sides of the case eagerly anticipate my every word because what I say (and don't say) can sometimes be an integral part of what wins or loses the case. Because I am required to narrow my response to only to the question asked by the opposing attorney, the possibility exists for me to respond in a way that will mislead the court. Because the attorneys on both sides know everything about their side of the case—including the strengths and weaknesses—I am carefully watched for what I say and don't say. Because of the *shades of gray* in highly complex matters that only the attorney and I know about, it would be easy for me to "tip the scales" with my words. But I don't do that because, after the case has been won or lost and all the money and other resources at stake have been shuffled between the winning and losing parties, I will only remember I chose to "tell the truth, the whole truth, so help me God."

Similar situations have occurred outside court. When I work as a consultant reviewing testing and hiring practices, I sometimes uncover tests or employment practices that are discriminatory and violate federal civil rights laws. When I bring this "bad news" to the attention of the company, I am often met with mixed responses. Sometimes the client will discontinue our services, and I'll never hear from them again (sort of a "shoot the messenger" response); other times our company can end up being an integral part of the solution that reaps rewards for everyone involved.

I've also encountered situations in my career where I've needed to take ethical stands on issues in which others do not agree. Some of the articles I've written in the area of civil rights and equal employment opportunity have been met with strong opposition, but I believe my perspectives were in line with both Scripture and the "law of the land." When taking these stands, I've risked both my own reputation and our company's, but standing up to what is right has always served me best. In fact, it's been quite amazing how my willingness to take a stand on these issues has helped bring in the type of projects we should be working on and *screen out* the projects that don't fit the mold of the type of work we should be doing. Taking a stand on these issues has worked out to be a natural pruning process.

Would you rather please people by fitting truth into a mold that pleases them or please God by "saying it like it is" and coming away with a clear conscience? There are short-term and long-term consequences with each choice. A wise preacher once said, "Obey God. Blame Him for the consequences." When it comes to being truthful, this advice fits well.

Godly Men and Women Practice WYSIWYG (What You See Is What You Get)

Proverbs:

- "He who conceals his hatred has lying lips, and whoever spreads slander is a fool" (10:18).
- "The integrity of the upright guides them, but the unfaithful are destroyed by their duplicity" (11:3).
- "A wicked man puts up a bold front, but an upright man gives thought to his ways" (21:29).
- "A malicious man disguises himself with his lips, but in his heart he harbors deceit. Though his speech is charming, do not believe him, for seven abominations fill his heart. His malice may be concealed by deception, but his wickedness will be exposed in the assembly" (26:24-26).
- "Better is open rebuke than hidden love" (27:5).

My wife is one of the most godly people I know. One of the reasons I feel this way is because of her *transparency*. If she's upset, I know it (or will soon know it); if she's angry, her expression is clear; if overjoyed, she beams. I honestly believe she isn't even capable of being two-faced because it's not in her wiring. She wears her feelings on her sleeve, and this is one of the true beauties of her character.

These qualities are also checked with a real humility—she would be the first to say these qualities are the Lord's work rather than her own. She didn't acquire them by reading books or going to classes or attending counseling. She gained them by submitting her spirit daily to God's changing power and by following the godly example of other women.

I have personally been blessed in numerous ways by being married to a woman who is sincere and open. One of the blessings is in the area of communication, which is *simplified* and *effective*. There are no hidden agendas, no planned schemes, no false pretenses. I always know where I stand with her. We don't waste time dwelling on issues that aren't good for us. It is truly amazing how sincerity and forthrightness can effectively direct your life by eliminating negative issues—much in the same way a fire extinguisher can put out fires.

Another benefit to our marriage that comes from my wife's sincerity is having less stress—both in our relationship and our lives individually. Being open about the values, beliefs, convictions and passions we share avoids "crossing wires" in social interactions. It also serves to attract the people with whom we should form deeper connections and repel those we shouldn't. Don't get me wrong here— for God does not want stuffy and self-righteous followers who don't spend time with all kinds of people. Indeed, Christ Himself spent more time with "sinners" and "the lowly" during His life on earth than with the "righteous." The point is that "bad company corrupts good character" (1 Corinthians 15:33) because sometimes the best in all of us can be corrupted by people with whom we interact. If we're not open and forthright about our beliefs and convictions, we will wind up stringing along relationships that hinder our lives and don't help theirs.

Sometimes God may want to prune certain relationships from our lives. Being open and honest with others about our convictions and values leads us to a place in our lives that will bring us (and those around us) into blessing. By not being transparent about our convictions, we rob ourselves of blessings by passively "going with the flow" and living lives of half-resolve and lukewarm passion.

Now let's take a look at how sincerity and openness can play out in the business world. In the workplace countless benefits are enjoyed by being open, forthright and sincere. I've had the fortunate opportunity of meeting hundreds of executives and other business leaders in the corporate world, and I have paid close attention to how they differ on this issue. As a young professional, I recall being shocked at how candid and "straight-shooting" some of them were—even to the point of being "nearly rude." Even leaders with lives marked with integrity and effectiveness seemed to be pushy and frank when challenging issues and the people behind them.

It wasn't until years later that I began to understand why they acted this way. If they didn't deal with the issue head-on, the matter could continue, gain even more momentum and circle right back to hit them again. These leaders had obviously experienced several such situations and had eventually learned "the buck stops here." By being frank and candid with significant matters, they were being real and were passing on the gravity and the responsibility of the issue to their subordinates. Being candid ultimately made their jobs *easier* and made their subordinates *more effective*—which made everything *better overall*.

Another benefit that comes from being sincere is that it leaves little room for gossip. After dealing with the matter head-on *with those involved*, there is no need to go around gossiping. The flames and smoke of the issue will have already been extinguished by putting the water at the base of the fire—the very source of the matter. So many times I've been in difficult business deals that could have been resolved easily if all parties had been open, honest and sincere at the beginning of the interaction.

Proverbs uses strong language on the topic of sincerity and openness. With verses like "He who conceals his hatred has lying lips, and whoever spreads slander is a fool" (10:18) and "The integrity of the upright guides them, but the unfaithful are destroyed by their duplicity" (11:3), we ought to regard this as a serious matter and a true essential for living a life ruled by wisdom.

Being Known by God

Proverbs:

- "All a man's ways seem innocent to him, but motives are weighed by the Lord" (16:2).
- "The lamp of the Lord searches the spirit of a man; it searches out his inmost being" (20:27).
- "All a man's ways seem right to him, but the Lord weighs the heart" (21:2).
- "As water reflects a face, so a man's heart reflects the man" (27:19).

God wants *complete intimacy* with His children because He wants the relationship to be mutual, voluntary and fruitful for both parties. No relationship, however, can reach a level of true intimacy without sincerity and openness. Trying to have an intimate relationship with God or another person without sincerity is like trying to bake bread without using flour—sincerity is a fundamental ingredient for forming intimate relationships with others.

Lack of sincerity can hinder our relationship with God in the same way it can hinder our relationships with others. Lack of sincerity can stop intimacy from growing and erode the intimacy two have already developed. This can happen quickly and in a way that goes almost totally unnoticed. When two people in a relationship are not sincere, open and honest, the relationship will surely suffer in the short run and perish in the long run if it continues.

God desires to have a *passionate* and *real* connection with each of His children. Consider these reasons why.

He made each of us as unique individuals.

- "Are not two sparrows sold for a penny? Yet not one of them will fall to the ground apart from the will of your Father. And even the very hairs of your head are all numbered. So don't be afraid; you are worth more than many sparrows" (Matthew 10:29-31).
- "For you created my inmost being; you knit me together in my mother's womb. I praise you because I am fearfully and wonderfully made; your works are wonderful, I know that full well. My frame was not hidden from you when I was made in the secret place. When I was woven together in the depths of the earth, your eyes saw my unformed body. All the days ordained for me were written in your book before one of them came to be" (Psalm 139:13-16).

God regularly scans our hearts—as if through an X-ray machine—to see where we are spiritually.

- "For the eyes of the Lord range throughout the earth to strengthen those whose hearts are fully committed to him" (2 Chronicles 16:9).
- "Search me, O God, and know my heart; test me and know my anxious thoughts. See if there is any offensive way in me, and lead me in the way everlasting" (Psalm 139:23-24).
- "O Lord, you have searched me and you know me. You know when I sit and when I rise; you perceive my thoughts from afar. You discern my going out and my lying down; you are familiar with all my ways. Before a word is on my tongue you know it completely, O Lord" (Psalm 139:1-4).
- "But the Lord said to Samuel, 'Do not consider his appearance or his height, for I have rejected him. The Lord does not look at the things man looks at. Man looks at the

outward appearance, but the Lord looks at the heart'" (1 Samuel 7:14).

He wants us to volunteer our innermost selves to Him and to strive to develop an intimate relationship with Him so we will willingly volunteer our time, strength and obedience to Him.

- "Now we see but a poor reflection as in a mirror; then we shall see face to face. Now I know in part; then I shall know fully, even as I am fully known" (1 Corinthians 13:12).
- "May the words of my mouth and the meditation of my heart be pleasing in your sight, O Lord, my Rock and my Redeemer" (Psalm 19:14).
- "I will instruct you and teach you in the way you should go; I will counsel you and watch over you. Do not be like the horse or the mule, which have no understanding but must be controlled by bit and bridle or they will not come to you" (Psalm 32:8-9).

You are in a relationship with God right now. What type of relationship is it? Is it marked by openness, truth and sincerity? Are there any blocks in the way? If so, they need to be cleared using prayer and, in some cases, repentance. We need to do *whatever it takes* to maintain the most important relationship in our lives.

References

Barton, B. B., & Veerman, D. R. (1992). *James: Life Application Bible Commentary*. Wheaton, IL: Tyndale House Publishers.

Gaebelein, F. E. (1982). *The Expositor's Bible Commentary* (Volume 5). Grand Rapids, MI: Zondervan.

Hubbard, D. (1989). *Mastering the Old Testament* (Volume 15A: Proverbs). Dallas, TX: Word Publishing.

Johnston, R. (2005), personal communication, December 29, 2005. Dr. Johnston is professor of New Testament and Christian Origins at Andrews University, Seventh Day Adventist Theological Seminary.

Kempis, T. (1998). *The Imitation of Christ*. New York, NY: Vintage Press.

Koptak, P. E. (2003). *Proverbs: NIV Application Commentary*. Grand Rapids, MI: Zondervan.

McCartney, D. G. (Fall, 2000). *The Wisdom of James the Just*. Southern Baptist Journal of Theology, 4 (3) (p. 53, footnotes omitted).

Murphy, R. E. (1998). *Proverbs. World Biblical Commentary.* Thomas Nelson Inc.

Nystrom, D. (1997). *The NIV Application Commentary: James.* Grand Rapids, MI: Zondervan.

Swindoll, C. (November 8, 2006). *God Expects Us to Love Kindness.* Audio Recording: Insight for Living.

Waltke, B. K. (2005). The Book of Proverbs: Chapters 15-31 (New International Commentary on the Old Testament). Grand Rapids, MI: Wm. B. Eerdmans Publishing Company.

Appendix

The River Wisdom

Wisdom revealed by the Lord's own creation
She shows her ways by the river...

She is First of all Pure...

First she receives all that is pure
Crystalline thoughts from above
Sophisticated beyond understanding
But all with the simplicity of pure love
They collect on our mind
Like the snowcapped mountains
Moved into action by His Son
In proper time

Briskly moved through her destined channel
Impurities removed
By the turmoil of her surroundings
So our intentions are refined
By the turbulence of life

Purity is only sustained
As we give all that we receive
And live, move, and breathe in His Way
By this we avoid the murky waters of stagnation
We must flow to others all we have received
As we move as He directs us

continued

As a river becomes a lake with no boundaries
Her depths fill with the impure
So our lives become
Without giving to others
And submitting to God's Way
And His Word

Then Peaceable...

She moves through wrong doing
The obstacles that block her way
Through the gentleness of true strength
Evoked only by the True Power
The insurmountable force behind her
Peace finds her way

A river enjoys peace within her borders
Knowing that her only power
And only hope of reaching her destination
Is to stay within her shape
So we enjoy peace
Within ours

Then Considerate and Gentle...

The power of a river is concealed
Masked by playful complexion and feathery rows
Yielding power to move boulders and carve canyons
All by flowing from the power above her, the Source
But a stream is dried as it departs from its Source
So our power is only kept
By staying with Him

We join with Wisdom's intention
By pouring our strength into another
Without return from our receiver
But only replenishment from the Source

Investing energy and life into causes
With results never seen

Then Submissive and Willing to Yield...

A river will ultimately accomplish her purpose
Flowing around obstacles
She does not calculate her ways
But moves and flows
As the Power above guides her

Sometimes she yields
Only to allow the time of her pressure
To move the block
Realizing no sudden force of will
Will move the way
But only the directed power from Above
And time

She has no self will
Only the strength of the Force behind her
She does not fight back
She flows only one direction
She passes by the channels that would dry her way
She stays the course leading her to the elected purpose
To flow downstream and to nourish

Then Full of Mercy...

A river is relieving to the tired traveler
She brings tenderness to the wounded soul
Precious thoughts of recovering hope
To those who sit by her side
And listen

And Good Fruit...

continued

The river wisdom nourishes all she touches
She can be guided
She can be moved
Or she can be restrained

She always brings plenty and harvest
For those who tap her
She brings fruitfulness
She is the only way
To her plenty

And Impartial...

For *all* who chart her course and keep her bounds
Wisdom brings joy and safe travel
But she allows treachery to those who challenge her ways
Or those who mistake her grace and beauty
To be void of power and justice

And Sincere...

A refined mountain stream
Cleansed by challenges forced through
Her actions are marked
By the clarity of perfect love
And the beauty of seasoned intention
Giving unceasingly
Although sometimes forsaken

"There is a river whose streams make glad the city of God, the holy place where the Most High dwells"—Psalms 46:4

My Personal Testimony

When I was eleven years old I made a decision that changed my life forever. I chose to receive Jesus Christ as my personal Lord and Savior. Little did I know at the time that the decision I made would take me through some difficult times to follow. As my teenage years ensued, I began making some wrong choices. In fact, I made several. The poor decisions I made regarding my friends, morality and ethics soon took me down a road that was leading straight to destruction. Then, when I turned seventeen, I finally came to my senses after my parents showed me the door (and a few brick walls too). Thank God for them.

At that critical juncture I realized all I had was Christ. All of my other foundations had shattered—friends, money, relationships and everything else besides Christ—had let me down. I thank God for these difficult times because they opened my eyes to something I never would have learned without them—the fact that Christ is the only solid foundation on which to build my life.

And so I began putting Christ first in my life. Slowly I began dropping habits, sins and relationships that drew me away from God's best and started making choices governed by God's Word. I started building my life using *His blueprint*—the Bible. Four short years later the Lord blessed me with a wife who was out of my league—a true woman of God. As we committed to put God first in our lives and order our lives after His best, the blessings (and challenges) continued. Over a period of eight years He blessed us with four incredible children. All are a testament to God's grace and blessing. All will continue Christ's redemption of my life into theirs—for hundreds of generations to come.

Leaving no area of my life untouched, He has also blessed my work and business in unimaginable ways. He has shown me He wants headship in this area, as I take second seat in the pilot's cabin. He has also shown me that being a minister and ambassador for Christ isn't limited to working in the church. I have applied the wisdom principles in His Word to my life and continue to be amazed at how well they work.

Therefore everyone who hears these words of mine and puts them into practice is like a wise man who built his house on the rock. The rain came down, the streams rose, and the winds blew and beat against that house; yet it did not fall, because it had its foundation on the rock. But everyone who hears these words of mine and does not put them into practice is like a foolish man who built his house on sand. The rain came down, the streams rose, and the winds blew and beat against that house, and it fell with a great crash. When Jesus had finished saying these things, the crowds were amazed at his teaching, because he taught as one who had authority, and not as their teachers of the law (Matthew 7:24-29).

The Seven Pillars of Wisdom

A photo of the Seven Pillars of Wisdom from the Sopoćani Monastery, a foundation of King Urosh I, which was built in the second half of the thirteenth century near the source of the river Raška in the region of Ras, the center of the Serbian medieval state.

This book does not claim God used the writers of the original biblical texts to secretly encapsulate seven traits of godly wisdom in a few verses of Scripture (James 3:17 and Proverbs 9:1). But the position is taken that James *intentionally* chose the seven primary aspects of godly wisdom. Further, when these seven pillars are used to categorize the seemingly random assortment of 915 verses in Proverbs, it provides a remarkably organized framework.

How do we know the seven qualities of wisdom listed by James include the key, primary qualities of wisdom? Did he leave any out? Surely it can be argued godly wisdom has numerous other aspects—truth, honesty, character, work ethic, discipline, integrity, knowledge, tact and others—but these are not included. James deliberately lists these seven as the key elements of godly wisdom.

There are three reasons that explain why James was intentional about listing only these seven attributes of godly wisdom. First, Scripture interprets Scripture, and using the book of James to unpack the seven pillars of wisdom seems reasonable. Second, there are remarkable connections between the book of James and Proverbs. Of all sixty-six books in the Bible, these two share important commonalities. Third, the literary structure of James 3:17 is *absolutely intentional*, leaving little room to believe James was pulling each of the seven wisdom characteristics out of thin air or simply writing freely about the topic. Each of these reasons is discussed in more detail below.

Scripture Interprets Scripture

Scripture passages should be interpreted in light of other Scripture passages that speak on similar topics. Applying this principle to James 3:17, it is not a coincidence he lists purity and seven other key attributes of wisdom, while Proverbs 9:1 states there are *seven pillars of wisdom*. There has been much deliberation about what the "seven pillars" refer to in this Proverbs passage. Explanations range from symbols of the pillars of the earth, the seven Hebrew poems in Proverbs chapters 2-7 or the seven superscriptions in the book of Proverbs (1:1; 10:1; 22:17; 24:23; 25:1; 30:1; 31:1) (Koptak, 2003, p. 265).

While one or more of these explanations may carry some truth, the wisdom passage in Proverbs 9 provides a context for wisdom's *house* (including substance, hospitality and an invitation to all to enter), and Proverbs 9:1, the opening verse in this section, provides the basic structure of wisdom's house which is made up of these "seven pillars." Thinking about this from a construction standpoint, temples built in ancient times typically used seven pillars to support the inner structure: one on each corner (four total) and one in between each corner, except for the front entryway (three more), for seven pillars in all.

King Solomon was an expert architect. God entrusted him to design and build his own personal temple (1 Kings 5), so it is highly likely the seven pillars were chosen deliberately when he authored most of Proverbs. While King Solomon established these seven pillars in the book of Proverbs in about 930 B.C., James defines them about a thousand years later using a literary device called *assonance* so they would be memorable and significant (see below).

Proverbs and the Book of James

How familiar was James with the book of Proverbs? Was James thinking about the seven pillars of wisdom mentioned in Proverbs 9:1 when he penned the seven attributes of wisdom in James 3:17? McCartney (2000) provides some unique insights that help to answer these questions: "James knows and uses Proverbs. James 4:6 cites Proverbs 3:34, and James 5:20 alludes to Proverbs 10:12. To this we might add the echo of Proverbs 27:1 ("do not boast about tomorrow") in James 4:13-16 and many other parallels."

McCartney also points out that James seemed highly familiar with the ancient wisdom texts of his time: "At least 40 of the 108 verses of James have literary parallels in (biblical) wisdom literature. The language and style of James reflect wisdom origins. Of James's 67 New Testament *hapaxes* (a word that occurs only once in the written works of an author), 34 are found in the wisdom literature of the Septuagint (the oldest Greek version of the Old Testament) and of the 21 words that James shares with only one other New Testament author, 19 occur commonly in the biblical wisdom books."

This evidence makes it clear that James was intimately familiar with the wisdom books of the Bible—including Proverbs. In fact, the book of Proverbs is quoted only ten times in the entire New Testament (Gaebelein, 1982, 890). Two (or possibly three, as explained above) of these are cited by James in his relatively small book of only five chapters.

The Literary Structure of James 3:17

James intentionally used a memorable literary structure to list the seven "wisdom attributes" he provides in this passage. This means that each of the seven attributes and the order in which they are listed were deliberate. At least two biblical scholars have pointed out that James uses *assonance* when listing the wisdom attributes in James 3:17. Assonance is a literary device designed to encapsulate a passage into a memorable, rhythmic pattern, for example, "Fleet feet sweep by sleeping Greeks" and "Every time I write a rhyme, these people think it's a crime." Regarding this assonance, Dr. Robert Johnston (2005) explains:

> Regarding the literary structure of James 3:17, *Hagne* (moral purity) is presented by James as the capital adjective to which the other wisdom characteristics are subordinated. Therefore, it is the main characteristic of the wisdom from above. This term is then unpacked by a series of adjectives, and the fact that they are chosen partly for rhetorical reasons is revealed by their assonance: the first four all begin with the Greek letter *epsilon*, the fifth begins with *mu* but begins a phrase that ends with a key word beginning with *alpha*, and the last two begin with *alpha*, so that you have e-e-e-e-m>a-a-a. The words express very important concepts but they were chosen partly to fit into this literary device.

> Next we examine the series of seven adjectives. The first four, all beginning with *epsilon,* are single words. The fourth adjective, *meste* (full), begins a whole phrase, "full of mercy and good fruits." Then come two more single adjectives that begin with *alpha.* The last word in the phrase that began with *meste* is *agathwn*, which begins with *alpha* and immediately precedes the final two adjectives beginning with *alpha.*

Dr. David Nystrom (1997) outlines a similar observation about the literary structure of James 3:17.

Purity is listed first because in many ways it is the most important, paving the way for others. James has arranged the remaining seven virtues to employ assonance first with *e*, then with *a*: peace-loving (*Eirenikos*), considerate (*Epieikes*), submissive (*Eupeithes*), full of mercy (*Meste Eleos*), good fruit (*Karpon Agathon*), impartial (*Adiakritos*) and sincere (*Anupokrits*).

The three reasons discussed above indicate James was intentional about his listing of the seven wisdom attributes. But there is something more that makes the choice of seven wisdom characteristics an appealing interpretation: the fact that the seven attributes overlap nicely with other key parts of Scripture where believers are encouraged to "be a certain way." These are the passages written by the apostle Paul dealing with "the fruit of the Spirit," which are attributes that manifest in our lives by being filled with God's power (Galatians 5:22-23) and the characteristics of love in the famous love passage (1 Corinthians 13:4-7). The table below shows this overlap of the three Scripture passages.

Wisdom Attribute from James 3:17			
Wisdom Pillar (Greek Term)	**Greek Definition**	**Fruit of the Spirit (Gal. 5:22-23)**	**Love (1 Cor. 13)**
Peaceable (*Eirenikos*)	Relating to peace, loving peace, bringing peace with one's presence; with a focus of having freedom from emotional worry and frustration.	Peace, patience	Patient, not easily angered
Considerate (*Epieikes*)	Seemingly, suitable, equitable, fair, mild and gentle.	Kindness, love, gentleness	Kind, not envious, not self-seeking
Submissive /Humble (*Eupeithes*)	Easily obeying, compliant, submissive, obedient.	Patience, kindness, self control	Not boastful, not proud

Merciful (*Eleos*)	Kindness or good will toward the miserable and the afflicted; practicing the virtue of mercy; the moral quality of feeling compassion and especially showing kindness toward someone in need.	Love	Keeps no record of wrongs, not easily angered
Good Fruit (*Karpon Agathon)*	Fruit of the trees, vines, of the fields, the fruit of one's loins (children); an effect, result, work, act, deed, advantage, profit, a "reaped" harvest.	Goodness, faithfulness	Always protects, always trusts, always hopes, always perseveres
Impartial (*Adiakritos*)	Undistinguished, being without dubiousness, ambiguity or uncertainty; free from prejudice.	Self control	Does not delight in evil but rejoices with the truth
Sincere (*Anupokrits*)	Unfeigned, undisguised, genuine, without hypocrisy, of good character, lacking pretense and prideful show.	Love	Does not delight in evil but rejoices with the truth

Note. Greek definitions from Aland, B., & Metzger, B. (1993). *The Greek New Testament (UBS4) with Greek-English Dictionary.* American Bible Society: New York, NY.

According to the apostle Paul, the nine "fruits of the spirit" are divinely manifested in our lives when we stay connected to Christ. Anyone can fake these traits or exhibit them through human power for a time, but when these "fruits" are displayed in a believer's life in their purest, most unselfish form, they are the natural fruit produced in our lives by remaining in Christ.

John 15 says believers can bear much fruit in their lives if they stay connected to the vine (Christ), but without this connection we can do nothing of real lasting value. The fruits shown in the table above are the *natural response* of being connected to Christ (You've never seen an apple tree moan as it bears apples, have you?). We are influenced by the people with whom we share our time and heart.

Spending time with Christ—through devotion, prayer, worship—helps us become more like Him and demonstrate these characteristics in our lives in pure ways that have lasting effects.

Living a life of godly wisdom is done much in the same way—these seven attributes of wisdom become part of who we are as we seek to maintain a relationship with Christ. John 15 also says we can do nothing of real value unless we are connected to Christ. Galatians 5 says we can be filled with incredible virtues if we are continually filled with His Spirit. Godly wisdom is manifest in our lives in these same ways.

There is one more consideration about James's deliberate choice in selecting these seven key pillars of wisdom: They make good practical, common sense! Try putting these seven attributes through a test by asking: Would a Christian really be living a life marked by godly, biblical wisdom without *each one* of these qualities? These pillars make up a comprehensive list of the spiritual, Christ-like qualities by which He wants every Christian to live their lives.

Proverbs Included in the Seven Pillars

A total of 467 verses fall within the seven pillars. Some verses are listed on more than one wisdom pillar. Because each of the seven pillars is a "continuum" of a trait or behavior, some verses below are the opposite of the wisdom pillar.

Purity (the Foundation of Wisdom)

Verse	Proverb
1:20	Wisdom calls aloud in the street, she raises her voice in the public squares;
1:21	at the head of the noisy streets she cries out, in the gateways of the city she makes her speech:
1:22	"How long will you simple ones love your simple ways? How long will mockers delight in mockery and fools hate knowledge?
1:24	But since you rejected me when I called and no one gave heed when I stretched out my hand,
1:25	since you ignored all my advice and would not accept my rebuke,
1:26	I in turn will laugh at your disaster; I will mock when calamity overtakes you—

1:27	when calamity overtakes you like a storm, when disaster sweeps over you like a whirlwind, when distress and trouble overwhelm you.
1:28	"Then they will call to me but I will not answer; they will look for me but will not find me.
1:29	Since they hated knowledge and did not choose to fear the Lord,
1:30	since they would not accept my advice and spurned my rebuke,
1:31	they will eat the fruit of their ways and be filled with the fruit of their schemes.
1:32	For the waywardness of the simple will kill them, and the complacency of fools will destroy them;
1:33	but whoever listens to me will live in safety and be at ease, without fear of harm.
2:7	He holds victory in store for the upright, he is a shield to those whose walk is blameless,
2:8	for he guards the course of the just and protects the way of his faithful ones.
2:9	Then you will understand what is right and just and fair—every good path.
2:10	For wisdom will enter your heart, and knowledge will be pleasant to your soul.
2:11	Discretion will protect you, and understanding will guard you.
3:21	My son, preserve sound judgment and discernment, do not let them out of your sight;
3:22	they will be life for you, an ornament to grace your neck.
3:23	Then you will go on your way in safety, and your foot will not stumble;

3:24	when you lie down, you will not be afraid; when you lie down, your sleep will be sweet.
3:25	Have no fear of sudden disaster or of the ruin that overtakes the wicked,
3:26	for the Lord will be your confidence and will keep your foot from being snared.
3:31	Do not envy a violent man or choose any of his ways,
3:32	for the Lord detests a perverse man but takes the upright into his confidence.
3:33	The Lord's curse is on the house of the wicked, but he blesses the home of the righteous.
4:18	The path of the righteous is like the first gleam of dawn, shining ever brighter till the full light of day.
4:23	Above all else, guard your heart, for it is the wellspring of life.
4:24	Put away perversity from your mouth; keep corrupt talk far from your lips.
6:16	There are six things the Lord hates, seven that are detestable to him:
6:17	haughty eyes, a lying tongue, hands that shed innocent blood,
6:18	a heart that devises wicked schemes, feet that are quick to rush into evil,
6:19	a false witness who pours out lies and a man who stirs up dissension among brothers.
8:6	Listen, for I have worthy things to say; I open my lips to speak what is right.
8:7	My mouth speaks what is true, for my lips detest wickedness.
8:8	All the words of my mouth are just; none of them is crooked or perverse.

8:9	To the discerning all of them are right; they are faultless to those who have knowledge.
8:13	To fear the Lord is to hate evil; I hate pride and arrogance, evil behavior and perverse speech.
10:7	The memory of the righteous will be a blessing, but the name of the wicked will rot.
10:9	The man of integrity walks securely, but he who takes crooked paths will be found out.
10:30	The righteous will never be uprooted, but the wicked will not remain in the land.
11:1	The Lord abhors dishonest scales, but accurate weights are his delight.
11:4	Wealth is worthless in the day of wrath, but righteousness delivers from death.
11:5	The righteousness of the blameless makes a straight way for them, but the wicked are brought down by their own wickedness.
11:6	The righteousness of the upright delivers them, but the unfaithful are trapped by evil desires.
11:8	The righteous man is rescued from trouble, and it comes on the wicked instead.
11:19	The truly righteous man attains life, but he who pursues evil goes to his death.
11:20	The Lord detests men of perverse heart but he delights in those whose ways are blameless.
11:21	Be sure of this: The wicked will not go unpunished, but those who are righteous will go free.
12:7	Wicked men are overthrown and are no more, but the house of the righteous stands firm.
12:12	The wicked desire the plunder of evil men, but the root of the righteous flourishes.

12:21	No harm befalls the righteous, but the wicked have their fill of trouble.
13:5	The righteous hate what is false, but the wicked bring shame and disgrace.
13:6	Righteousness guards the man of integrity, but wickedness overthrows the sinner.
14:11	The house of the wicked will be destroyed, but the tent of the upright will flourish.
14:32	When calamity comes, the wicked are brought down, but even in death the righteous have a refuge.
14:34	Righteousness exalts a nation, but sin is a disgrace to any people.
15:8	The Lord detests the sacrifice of the wicked, but the prayer of the upright pleases him.
15:9	The Lord detests the way of the wicked but he loves those who pursue righteousness.
16:2	All a man's ways seem innocent to him, but motives are weighed by the Lord.
16:11	Honest scales and balances are from the Lord; all the weights in the bag are of his making.
17:3	The crucible for silver and the furnace for gold, but the Lord tests the heart.
17:20	A man of perverse heart does not prosper; he whose tongue is deceitful falls into trouble.
17:23	A wicked man accepts a bribe in secret to pervert the course of justice.
19:3	A man's own folly ruins his life, yet his heart rages against the Lord.
19:5	A false witness will not go unpunished, and he who pours out lies will not go free.
20:7	The righteous man leads a blameless life; blessed are his children after him.

20:8	When a king sits on his throne to judge, he winnows out all evil with his eyes.
20:9	Who can say, "I have kept my heart pure; I am clean and without sin?"
20:10	Differing weights and differing measures—the Lord detests them both.
20:11	Even a child is known by his actions, by whether his conduct is pure and right.
20:17	Food gained by fraud tastes sweet to a man, but he ends up with a mouth full of gravel.
20:23	The Lord detests differing weights, and dishonest scales do not please him.
20:30	Blows and wounds cleanse away evil, and beatings purge the inmost being.
21:8	The way of the guilty is devious, but the conduct of the innocent is upright.
22:6	Train a child in the way he should go, and when he is old he will not turn from it.
22:24	Do not make friends with a hot-tempered man, do not associate with one easily angered.
23:19	Listen, my son, and be wise, and keep your heart on the right path.
23:20	Do not join those who drink too much wine or gorge themselves on meat,
23:21	for drunkards and gluttons become poor, and drowsiness clothes them in rags.
23:29	Who has woe? Who has sorrow? Who has strife? Who has complaints? Who has needless bruises? Who has bloodshot eyes?
23:30	Those who linger over wine, who go to sample bowls of mixed wine.

23:31	Do not gaze at wine when it is red, when it sparkles in the cup, when it goes down smoothly!
23:32	In the end it bites like a snake and poisons like a viper.
23:33	Your eyes will see strange sights and your mind imagine confusing things.
23:34	You will be like one sleeping on the high seas, lying on top of the rigging.
23:35	"They hit me," you will say, "but I'm not hurt! They beat me, but I don't feel it! When will I wake up so I can find another drink?"
24:15	Do not lie in wait like an outlaw against a righteous man's house, do not raid his dwelling place;
24:16	for though a righteous man falls seven times, he rises again, but the wicked are brought down by calamity.
25:4	Remove the dross from the silver, and out comes material for the silversmith;
25:5	remove the wicked from the king's presence, and his throne will be established through righteousness.
27:22	Though you grind a fool in a mortar, grinding him like grain with a pestle, you will not remove his folly from him.
28:6	Better a poor man whose walk is blameless than a rich man whose ways are perverse.
28:9	If anyone turns a deaf ear to the law, even his prayers are detestable.
28:13	He who conceals his sins does not prosper, but whoever confesses and renounces them finds mercy.
28:14	Blessed is the man who always fears the Lord, but he who hardens his heart falls into trouble.
28:18	He whose walk is blameless is kept safe, but he whose ways are perverse will suddenly fall.

28:28	When the wicked rise to power, people go into hiding; but when the wicked perish, the righteous thrive.
29:2	When the righteous thrive, the people rejoice; when the wicked rule, the people groan.
29:13	The poor man and the oppressor have this in common: The Lord gives sight to the eyes of both.
30:5	"Every word of God is flawless; he is a shield to those who take refuge in him.

Peace-loving

Verse	Proverb
3:13	Blessed is the man who finds wisdom, the man who gains understanding,
3:14	for she is more profitable than silver and yields better returns than gold.
3:15	She is more precious than rubies; nothing you desire can compare with her.
3:16	Long life is in her right hand; in her left hand are riches and honor.
3:17	Her ways are pleasant ways, and all her paths are peace.
3:18	She is a tree of life to those who embrace her; those who lay hold of her will be blessed.
6:12	A scoundrel and villain, who goes about with a corrupt mouth,
6:13	who winks with his eye, signals with his feet and motions with his fingers,
6:14	who plots evil with deceit in his heart—he always stirs up dissension.

6:15	Therefore disaster will overtake him in an instant; he will suddenly be destroyed—without remedy.
10:19	When words are many, sin is not absent, but he who holds his tongue is wise.
12:18	Reckless words pierce like a sword, but the tongue of the wise brings healing.
12:20	There is deceit in the hearts of those who plot evil, but joy for those who promote peace.
13:10	Pride only breeds quarrels, but wisdom is found in those who take advice.
14:29	A patient man has great understanding, but a quick-tempered man displays folly.
14:30	A heart at peace gives life to the body, but envy rots the bones.
15:1	A gentle answer turns away wrath, but a harsh word stirs up anger.
15:18	A hot-tempered man stirs up dissension, but a patient man calms a quarrel.
15:30	A cheerful look brings joy to the heart, and good news gives health to the bones.
16:7	When a man's ways are pleasing to the Lord, he makes even his enemies live at peace with him.
16:23	A wise man's heart guides his mouth, and his lips promote instruction.
16:32	Better a patient man than a warrior, a man who controls his temper than one who takes a city.
17:1	Better a dry crust with peace and quiet than a house full of feasting, with strife.
17:14	Starting a quarrel is like breaching a dam; so drop the matter before a dispute breaks out.
17:19	He who loves a quarrel loves sin; he who builds a high gate invites destruction.

18:18	Casting the lot settles disputes and keeps strong opponents apart.
18:19	An offended brother is more unyielding than a fortified city, and disputes are like the barred gates of a citadel.
19:13	A foolish son is his father's ruin, and a quarrelsome wife is like a constant dripping.
19:23	The fear of the Lord leads to life: Then one rests content, untouched by trouble.
20:3	It is to a man's honor to avoid strife, but every fool is quick to quarrel.
21:9	Better to live on a corner of the roof than share a house with a quarrelsome wife.
21:14	A gift given in secret soothes anger, and a bribe concealed in the cloak pacifies great wrath.
21:19	Better to live in a desert than with a quarrelsome and ill-tempered wife.
22:10	Drive out the mocker, and out goes strife; quarrels and insults are ended.
25:24	Better to live on a corner of the roof than share a house with a quarrelsome wife.
26:4	Do not answer a fool according to his folly, or you will be like him yourself.
26:5	Answer a fool according to his folly, or he will be wise in his own eyes.
26:17	Like one who seizes a dog by the ears is a passer-by who meddles in a quarrel not his own.
26:20	Without wood a fire goes out; without gossip a quarrel dies down.
26:21	As charcoal to embers and as wood to fire, so is a quarrelsome man for kindling strife.
29:17	Discipline your son, and he will give you peace; he will bring delight to your soul.

Considerate

Verse	Proverb
3:27	Do not withhold good from those who deserve it, when it is in your power to act.
3:28	Do not say to your neighbor, "Come back later; I'll give it tomorrow"—when you now have it with you.
10:21	The lips of the righteous nourish many, but fools die for lack of judgment.
11:16	A kindhearted woman gains respect, but ruthless men gain only wealth.
11:17	A kind man benefits himself, but a cruel man brings trouble on himself.
11:25	A generous man will prosper; he who refreshes others will himself be refreshed.
13:2	From the fruit of his lips a man enjoys good things, but the unfaithful have a craving for violence.
14:21	He who despises his neighbor sins, but blessed is he who is kind to the needy.
14:22	Do not those who plot evil go astray? But those who plan what is good find love and faithfulness.
17:17	A friend loves at all times, and a brother is born for adversity.
18:16	A gift opens the way for the giver and ushers him into the presence of the great.
18:24	A man of many companions may come to ruin, but there is a friend who sticks closer than a brother.
19:17	He who is kind to the poor lends to the Lord, and he will reward him for what he has done.
21:13	If a man shuts his ears to the cry of the poor, he too will cry out and not be answered.

22:2	Rich and poor have this in common: The Lord is the Maker of them all.
22:9	A generous man will himself be blessed, for he shares his food with the poor.
22:22	Do not exploit the poor because they are poor and do not crush the needy in court,
22:23	for the Lord will take up their case and will plunder those who plunder them.
23:10	Do not move an ancient boundary stone or encroach on the fields of the fatherless,
23:11	for their Defender is strong; he will take up their case against you.
24:11	Rescue those being led away to death; hold back those staggering toward slaughter.
24:12	If you say, "But we knew nothing about this," does not he who weighs the heart perceive it? Does not he who guards your life know it? Will he not repay each person according to what he has done?
24:17	Do not gloat when your enemy falls; when he stumbles, do not let your heart rejoice,
24:18	or the Lord will see and disapprove and turn his wrath away from him.
25:17	Seldom set foot in your neighbor's house—too much of you, and he will hate you.
25:20	Like one who takes away a garment on a cold day, or like vinegar poured on soda, is one who sings songs to a heavy heart.
25:25	Like cold water to a weary soul is good news from a distant land.
27:6	Wounds from a friend can be trusted, but an enemy multiplies kisses.
27:8	Like a bird that strays from its nest is a man who strays from his home.

27:9	Perfume and incense bring joy to the heart, and the pleasantness of one's friend springs from his earnest counsel.
27:10	Do not forsake your friend and the friend of your father, and do not go to your brother's house when disaster strikes you—better a neighbor nearby than a brother far away.
27:11	Be wise, my son, and bring joy to my heart; then I can answer anyone who treats me with contempt.
27:14	If a man loudly blesses his neighbor early in the morning, it will be taken as a curse.
27:15	A quarrelsome wife is like a constant dripping on a rainy day;
27:16	restraining her is like restraining the wind or grasping oil with the hand.
27:17	As iron sharpens iron, so one man sharpens another.
28:3	A ruler who oppresses the poor is like a driving rain that leaves no crops.
28:15	Like a roaring lion or a charging bear is a wicked man ruling over a helpless people.
28:27	He who gives to the poor will lack nothing, but he who closes his eyes to them receives many curses.
29:7	The righteous care about justice for the poor, but the wicked have no such concern.
29:14	If a king judges the poor with fairness, his throne will always be secure.
31:8	"Speak up for those who cannot speak for themselves, for the rights of all who are destitute.
31:9	Speak up and judge fairly; defend the rights of the poor and needy."
31:20	She opens her arms to the poor and extends her hands to the needy.

31:21	When it snows, she has no fear for her household; for all of them are clothed in scarlet.
31:22	She makes coverings for her bed; she is clothed in fine linen and purple.

Submissive

Verse	Proverb
1:7	The fear of the Lord is the beginning of knowledge, but fools despise wisdom and discipline.
2:1	My son, if you accept my words and store up my commands within you,
2:2	turning your ear to wisdom and applying your heart to understanding,
2:3	and if you call out for insight and cry aloud for understanding,
2:4	and if you look for it as for silver and search for it as for hidden treasure,
2:5	then you will understand the fear of the Lord and find the knowledge of God.
3:5	Trust in the Lord with all your heart and lean not on your own understanding;
3:6	in all your ways acknowledge him, and he will make your paths straight.
3:7	Do not be wise in your own eyes; fear the Lord and shun evil.
3:8	This will bring health to your body and nourishment to your bones.
3:34	He mocks proud mockers but gives grace to the humble.
3:35	The wise inherit honor, but fools he holds up to shame.

6:1	My son, if you have put up security for your neighbor, if you have struck hands in pledge for another,
6:2	if you have been trapped by what you said, ensnared by the words of your mouth,
6:3	then do this, my son, to free yourself, since you have fallen into your neighbor's hands: Go and humble yourself; press your plea with your neighbor!
6:4	Allow no sleep to your eyes, no slumber to your eyelids.
6:5	Free yourself, like a gazelle from the hand of the hunter, like a bird from the snare of the fowler.
8:13	To fear the Lord is to hate evil; I hate pride and arrogance, evil behavior and perverse speech.
9:8	Do not rebuke a mocker or he will hate you; rebuke a wise man and he will love you.
9:9	Instruct a wise man and he will be wiser still; teach a righteous man and he will add to his learning.
9:10	"The fear of the Lord is the beginning of wisdom, and knowledge of the Holy One is understanding.
10:8	The wise in heart accept commands, but a chattering fool comes to ruin.
10:17	He who heeds discipline shows the way to life, but whoever ignores correction leads others astray.
11:2	When pride comes, then comes disgrace, but with humility comes wisdom.
11:14	For lack of guidance a nation falls, but many advisers make victory sure.
12:1	Whoever loves discipline loves knowledge, but he who hates correction is stupid.
12:15	The way of a fool seems right to him, but a wise man listens to advice.
12:16	A fool shows his annoyance at once, but a prudent man overlooks an insult.

13:10	Pride only breeds quarrels, but wisdom is found in those who take advice.
13:18	He who ignores discipline comes to poverty and shame, but whoever heeds correction is honored.
15:5	A fool spurns his father's discipline, but whoever heeds correction shows prudence.
15:10	Stern discipline awaits him who leaves the path; he who hates correction will die.
15:12	A mocker resents correction; he will not consult the wise.
15:22	Plans fail for lack of counsel, but with many advisers they succeed.
15:25	The Lord tears down the proud man's house but he keeps the widow's boundaries intact.
15:31	He who listens to a life-giving rebuke will be at home among the wise.
15:32	He who ignores discipline despises himself, but whoever heeds correction gains understanding.
15:33	The fear of the Lord teaches a man wisdom, and humility comes before honor.
16:5	The Lord detests all the proud of heart. Be sure of this: They will not go unpunished.
16:9	In his heart a man plans his course, but the Lord determines his steps.
16:18	Pride goes before destruction, a haughty spirit before a fall.
16:19	Better to be lowly in spirit and among the oppressed than to share plunder with the proud.
16:20	Whoever gives heed to instruction prospers, and blessed is he who trusts in the Lord.
17:10	A rebuke impresses a man of discernment more than a hundred lashes a fool.

18:12	Before his downfall a man's heart is proud, but humility comes before honor.
18:17	The first to present his case seems right, till another comes forward and questions him.
19:2	It is not good to have zeal without knowledge, nor to be hasty and miss the way.
19:11	A man's wisdom gives him patience; it is to his glory to overlook an offense.
19:16	He who obeys instructions guards his life, but he who is contemptuous of his ways will die.
19:20	Listen to advice and accept instruction, and in the end you will be wise.
19:25	Flog a mocker, and the simple will learn prudence; rebuke a discerning man, and he will gain knowledge.
20:6	Many a man claims to have unfailing love, but a faithful man who can find?
20:18	Make plans by seeking advice; if you wage war, obtain guidance.
21:4	Haughty eyes and a proud heart, the lamp of the wicked, are sin!
21:11	When a mocker is punished, the simple gain wisdom; when a wise man is instructed, he gets knowledge.
21:24	The proud and arrogant man—"Mocker" is his name; he behaves with overweening pride.
22:4	Humility and the fear of the Lord bring wealth and honor and life.
24:5	A wise man has great power, and a man of knowledge increases strength;
24:6	for waging war you need guidance, and for victory many advisers.
25:6	Do not exalt yourself in the king's presence, and do not claim a place among great men;

25:7	it is better for him to say to you, "Come up here," than for him to humiliate you before a nobleman.
25:8	What you have seen with your eyes do not bring hastily to court, for what will you do in the end if your neighbor puts you to shame?
25:12	Like an earring of gold or an ornament of fine gold is a wise man's rebuke to a listening ear.
25:27	It is not good to eat too much honey, nor is it honorable to seek one's own honor.
26:12	Do you see a man wise in his own eyes? There is more hope for a fool than for him.
27:2	Let another praise you, and not your own mouth; someone else, and not your own lips.
27:17	As iron sharpens iron, so one man sharpens another.
27:21	The crucible for silver and the furnace for gold, but man is tested by the praise he receives.
28:26	He who trusts in himself is a fool, but he who walks in wisdom is kept safe.
29:1	A man who remains stiff-necked after many rebukes will suddenly be destroyed—without remedy.
29:11	A fool gives full vent to his anger, but a wise man keeps himself under control.
29:23	A man's pride brings him low, but a man of lowly spirit gains honor.

Merciful

Verse	Proverb
8:20	I walk in the way of righteousness, along the paths of justice.

10:12	Hatred stirs up dissension, but love covers over all wrongs.
13:24	He who spares the rod hates his son, but he who loves him is careful to discipline him.
14:31	He who oppresses the poor shows contempt for their Maker, but whoever is kind to the needy honors God.
16:8	Better a little with righteousness than much gain with injustice.
16:10	The lips of a king speak as an oracle, and his mouth should not betray justice.
17:5	He who mocks the poor shows contempt for their Maker; whoever gloats over disaster will not go unpunished.
17:9	He who covers over an offense promotes love, but whoever repeats the matter separates close friends.
17:15	Acquitting the guilty and condemning the innocent—the Lord detests them both.
17:26	It is not good to punish an innocent man, or to flog officials for their integrity.
18:5	It is not good to be partial to the wicked or to deprive the innocent of justice.
18:23	A poor man pleads for mercy, but a rich man answers harshly.
21:13	If a man shuts his ears to the cry of the poor, he too will cry out and not be answered.
21:15	When justice is done, it brings joy to the righteous but terror to evildoers.
22:22	Do not exploit the poor because they are poor and do not crush the needy in court,
22:23	for the Lord will take up their case and will plunder those who plunder them.

23:13	Do not withhold discipline from a child; if you punish him with the rod, he will not die!
23:14	Punish him with the rod and save his soul from death.
24:17	Do not gloat when your enemy falls; when he stumbles, do not let your heart rejoice,
24:18	or the Lord will see and disapprove and turn his wrath away from him.
24:28	Do not testify against your neighbor without cause, or use your lips to deceive.
24:29	Do not say, "I'll do to him as he has done to me; I'll pay that man back for what he did."
25:21	If your enemy is hungry, give him food to eat; if he is thirsty, give him water to drink.
25:22	In doing this, you will heap burning coals on his head, and the Lord will reward you.
28:5	Evil men do not understand justice, but those who seek the Lord understand it fully.
29:7	The righteous care about justice for the poor, but the wicked have no such concern.
29:26	Many seek an audience with a ruler, but it is from the Lord that man gets justice.
31:8	"Speak up for those who cannot speak for themselves, for the rights of all who are destitute.
31:9	Speak up and judge fairly; defend the rights of the poor and needy."

Fruitful

Verse	Proverb
2:6	For the Lord gives wisdom, and from his mouth come knowledge and understanding.
2:7	He holds victory in store for the upright, he is a shield to those whose walk is blameless,
2:8	for he guards the course of the just and protects the way of his faithful ones.
2:9	Then you will understand what is right and just and fair—every good path.
2:10	For wisdom will enter your heart, and knowledge will be pleasant to your soul.
2:11	Discretion will protect you, and understanding will guard you.
2:12	Wisdom will save you from the ways of wicked men, from men whose words are perverse,
2:13	who leave the straight paths to walk in dark ways,
2:14	who delight in doing wrong and rejoice in the perverseness of evil,
2:15	whose paths are crooked and who are devious in their ways.
2:16	It will save you also from the adulteress, from the wayward wife with her seductive words,
2:17	who has left the partner of her youth and ignored the covenant she made before God.
2:18	For her house leads down to death and her paths to the spirits of the dead.
2:19	None who go to her return or attain the paths of life.
2:20	Thus you will walk in the ways of good men and keep to the paths of the righteous.

2:21	For the upright will live in the land, and the blameless will remain in it;
2:22	but the wicked will be cut off from the land, and the unfaithful will be torn from it.
3:1	My son, do not forget my teaching, but keep my commands in your heart,
3:2	for they will prolong your life many years and bring you prosperity.
3:3	Let love and faithfulness never leave you; bind them around your neck, write them on the tablet of your heart.
3:4	Then you will win favor and a good name in the sight of God and man.
3:5	Trust in the Lord with all your heart and lean not on your own understanding;
3:6	in all your ways acknowledge him, and he will make your paths straight.
3:7	Do not be wise in your own eyes; fear the Lord and shun evil.
3:8	This will bring health to your body and nourishment to your bones.
3:9	Honor the Lord with your wealth, with the firstfruits of all your crops;
3:10	then your barns will be filled to overflowing, and your vats will brim over with new wine.
3:13	Blessed is the man who finds wisdom, the man who gains understanding,
3:14	for she is more profitable than silver and yields better returns than gold.
3:15	She is more precious than rubies; nothing you desire can compare with her.
3:16	Long life is in her right hand; in her left hand are riches and honor.

3:17	Her ways are pleasant ways, and all her paths are peace.
3:18	She is a tree of life to those who embrace her; those who lay hold of her will be blessed.
3:19	By wisdom the Lord laid the earth's foundations, by understanding he set the heavens in place;
3:20	by his knowledge the deeps were divided, and the clouds let drop the dew.
3:21	My son, preserve sound judgment and discernment, do not let them out of your sight;
3:22	they will be life for you, an ornament to grace your neck.
3:23	Then you will go on your way in safety, and your foot will not stumble;
3:24	when you lie down, you will not be afraid; when you lie down, your sleep will be sweet.
3:25	Have no fear of sudden disaster or of the ruin that overtakes the wicked,
3:26	for the Lord will be your confidence and will keep your foot from being snared.
4:1	Listen, my sons, to a father's instruction; pay attention and gain understanding.
4:2	I give you sound learning, so do not forsake my teaching.
4:3	When I was a boy in my father's house, still tender, and an only child of my mother,
4:4	he taught me and said, "Lay hold of my words with all your heart; keep my commands and you will live.
4:5	Get wisdom, get understanding; do not forget my words or swerve from them.
4:6	Do not forsake wisdom, and she will protect you; love her, and she will watch over you.
4:7	Wisdom is supreme; therefore get wisdom. Though it cost all you have, get understanding.

4:8	Esteem her, and she will exalt you; embrace her, and she will honor you.
4:9	She will set a garland of grace on your head and present you with a crown of splendor."
4:10	Listen, my son, accept what I say, and the years of your life will be many.
4:11	I guide you in the way of wisdom and lead you along straight paths.
4:12	When you walk, your steps will not be hampered; when you run, you will not stumble.
4:20	My son, pay attention to what I say; listen closely to my words.
4:21	Do not let them out of your sight, keep them within your heart;
4:22	for they are life to those who find them and health to a man's whole body.
4:25	Let your eyes look straight ahead, fix your gaze directly before you.
4:26	Make level paths for your feet and take only ways that are firm.
4:27	Do not swerve to the right or the left; keep your foot from evil.
6:20	My son, keep your father's commands and do not forsake your mother's teaching.
6:21	Bind them upon your heart forever; fasten them around your neck.
6:22	When you walk, they will guide you; when you sleep, they will watch over you; when you awake, they will speak to you.
6:23	For these commands are a lamp, this teaching is a light, and the corrections of discipline are the way to life.
8:18	With me are riches and honor, enduring wealth and prosperity.

8:19	My fruit is better than fine gold; what I yield surpasses choice silver.
8:32	"Now then, my sons, listen to me; blessed are those who keep my ways.
8:33	Listen to my instruction and be wise; do not ignore it.
8:34	Blessed is the man who listens to me, watching daily at my doors, waiting at my doorway.
8:35	For whoever finds me finds life and receives favor from the Lord.
8:36	But whoever fails to find me harms himself; all who hate me love death."
9:11	For through me your days will be many, and years will be added to your life.
9:12	If you are wise, your wisdom will reward you; if you are a mocker, you alone will suffer."
10:22	The blessing of the Lord brings wealth, and he adds no trouble to it.
10:24	What the wicked dreads will overtake him; what the righteous desire will be granted.
10:27	The fear of the Lord adds length to life, but the years of the wicked are cut short.
10:28	The prospect of the righteous is joy, but the hopes of the wicked come to nothing.
11:11	Through the blessing of the upright a city is exalted, but by the mouth of the wicked it is destroyed.
11:18	The wicked man earns deceptive wages, but he who sows righteousness reaps a sure reward.
11:30	The fruit of the righteous is a tree of life, and he who wins souls is wise.
12:2	A good man obtains favor from the Lord, but the Lord condemns a crafty man.

12:24	Diligent hands will rule, but laziness ends in slave labor.
13:6	Righteousness guards the man of integrity, but wickedness overthrows the sinner.
13:13	He who scorns instruction will pay for it, but he who respects a command is rewarded.
13:15	Good understanding wins favor, but the way of the unfaithful is hard.
13:21	Misfortune pursues the sinner, but prosperity is the reward of the righteous.
14:14	The faithless will be fully repaid for their ways, and the good man rewarded for his.
14:26	He who fears the Lord has a secure fortress, and for his children it will be a refuge.
14:27	The fear of the Lord is a fountain of life, turning a man from the snares of death.
15:16	Better a little with the fear of the Lord than great wealth with turmoil.
15:21	Folly delights a man who lacks judgment, but a man of understanding keeps a straight course.
16:3	Commit to the Lord whatever you do, and your plans will succeed.
16:7	When a man's ways are pleasing to the Lord, he makes even his enemies live at peace with him.
16:16	How much better to get wisdom than gold, to choose understanding rather than silver!
16:25	There is a way that seems right to a man, but in the end it leads to death.
19:17	He who is kind to the poor lends to the Lord, and he will reward him for what he has done.
19:21	Many are the plans in a man's heart, but it is the Lord's purpose that prevails.

22:4	Humility and the fear of the Lord bring wealth and honor and life.
21:30	There is no wisdom, no insight, no plan that can succeed against the Lord.
21:31	The horse is made ready for the day of battle, but victory rests with the Lord.
24:15	Do not lie in wait like an outlaw against a righteous man's house, do not raid his dwelling place;
24:16	for though a righteous man falls seven times, he rises again, but the wicked are brought down by calamity.
28:10	He who leads the upright along an evil path will fall into his own trap, but the blameless will receive a good inheritance.
28:18	He whose walk is blameless is kept safe, but he whose ways are perverse will suddenly fall.
28:26	He who trusts in himself is a fool, but he who walks in wisdom is kept safe.
29:6	An evil man is snared by his own sin, but a righteous one can sing and be glad.
29:25	Fear of man will prove to be a snare, but whoever trusts in the Lord is kept safe.

Impartial

Verse	Proverb
1:23	If you had responded to my rebuke, I would have poured out my heart to you and made my thoughts known to you.
3:29	Do not plot harm against your neighbor, who lives trustfully near you.
3:30	Do not accuse a man for no reason—when he has done you no harm.

8:4	"To you, O men, I call out; I raise my voice to all mankind.
8:5	You who are simple, gain prudence; you who are foolish, gain understanding.
9:4	"Let all who are simple come in here!" she says to those who lack judgment.
11:1	The Lord abhors dishonest scales, but accurate weights are his delight.
16:10	The lips of a king speak as an oracle, and his mouth should not betray justice.
16:11	Honest scales and balances are from the Lord; all the weights in the bag are of his making.
17:15	Acquitting the guilty and condemning the innocent—the Lord detests them both.
18:5	It is not good to be partial to the wicked or to deprive the innocent of justice.
18:17	The first to present his case seems right, till another comes forward and questions him.
20:10	Differing weights and differing measures—the Lord detests them both.
20:11	Even a child is known by his actions, by whether his conduct is pure and right.
20:23	The Lord detests differing weights, and dishonest scales do not please him.
21:12	The Righteous One takes note of the house of the wicked and brings the wicked to ruin.
22:16	He who oppresses the poor to increase his wealth and he who gives gifts to the rich—both come to poverty.
24:23	These also are sayings of the wise: To show partiality in judging is not good:
24:24	Whoever says to the guilty, "You are innocent"—peoples will curse him and nations denounce him.

24:25	But it will go well with those who convict the guilty, and rich blessing will come upon them.
28:21	To show partiality is not good—yet a man will do wrong for a piece of bread.
28:23	He who rebukes a man will in the end gain more favor than he who has a flattering tongue.
29:13	The poor man and the oppressor have this in common: The Lord gives sight to the eyes of both.
29:14	If a king judges the poor with fairness, his throne will always be secure.
26:10	Like an archer who wounds at random is he who hires a fool or any passer-by.

Sincere

Verse	Proverb
6:12	A scoundrel and villain, who goes about with a corrupt mouth,
6:13	who winks with his eye, signals with his feet and motions with his fingers,
6:14	who plots evil with deceit in his heart—he always stirs up dissension.
6:15	Therefore disaster will overtake him in an instant; he will suddenly be destroyed—without remedy.
10:10	He who winks maliciously causes grief, and a chattering fool comes to ruin.
10:14	Wise men store up knowledge, but the mouth of a fool invites ruin.
10:18	He who conceals his hatred has lying lips, and whoever spreads slander is a fool.

11:3	The integrity of the upright guides them, but the unfaithful are destroyed by their duplicity.
11:13	A gossip betrays a confidence, but a trustworthy man keeps a secret.
12:17	A truthful witness gives honest testimony, but a false witness tells lies.
13:7	One man pretends to be rich, yet has nothing; another pretends to be poor, yet has great wealth.
12:22	The Lord detests lying lips, but he delights in men who are truthful.
14:5	A truthful witness does not deceive, but a false witness pours out lies.
14:25	A truthful witness saves lives, but a false witness is deceitful.
17:3	The crucible for silver and the furnace for gold, but the Lord tests the heart.
17:7	Arrogant lips are unsuited to a fool—how much worse lying lips to a ruler!
19:9	A false witness will not go unpunished, and he who pours out lies will perish.
19:28	A corrupt witness mocks at justice, and the mouth of the wicked gulps down evil.
20:14	"It's no good, it's no good!" says the buyer; then off he goes and boasts about his purchase.
20:25	It is a trap for a man to dedicate something rashly and only later to consider his vows.
20:27	The lamp of the Lord searches the spirit of a man; it searches out his inmost being.
21:2	All a man's ways seem right to him, but the Lord weighs the heart.

21:8	The way of the guilty is devious, but the conduct of the innocent is upright.
21:28	A false witness will perish, and whoever listens to him will be destroyed forever.
21:29	A wicked man puts up a bold front, but an upright man gives thought to his ways.
24:11	Rescue those being led away to death; hold back those staggering toward slaughter.
24:12	If you say, "But we knew nothing about this," does not he who weighs the heart perceive it? Does not he who guards your life know it? Will he not repay each person according to what he has done?
24:26	An honest answer is like a kiss on the lips.
25:9	If you argue your case with a neighbor, do not betray another man's confidence,
25:10	or he who hears it may shame you and you will never lose your bad reputation.
25:13	Like the coolness of snow at harvest time is a trustworthy messenger to those who send him; he refreshes the spirit of his masters.
25:14	Like clouds and wind without rain is a man who boasts of gifts he does not give.
25:18	Like a club or a sword or a sharp arrow is the man who gives false testimony against his neighbor.
25:23	As a north wind brings rain, so a sly tongue brings angry looks.
26:18	Like a madman shooting firebrands or deadly arrows
26:19	is a man who deceives his neighbor and says, "I was only joking!"
26:24	A malicious man disguises himself with his lips, but in his heart he harbors deceit.

26:25	Though his speech is charming, do not believe him, for seven abominations fill his heart.
26:26	His malice may be concealed by deception, but his wickedness will be exposed in the assembly.
26:28	A lying tongue hates those it hurts, and a flattering mouth works ruin.
27:5	Better is open rebuke than hidden love.
27:19	As water reflects a face, so a man's heart reflects the man.
28:11	A rich man may be wise in his own eyes, but a poor man who has discernment sees through him.
28:23	He who rebukes a man will in the end gain more favor than he who has a flattering tongue.
29:27	The righteous detest the dishonest; the wicked detest the upright.
31:30	Charm is deceptive, and beauty is fleeting; but a woman who fears the Lord is to be praised.

CPSIA information can be obtained
at www.ICGtesting.com
Printed in the USA
FFOW02n1748040214
3406FF